VOICES OF EXPERIENCE:
1500 Retired People Talk About Retirement

By Mario A. Milletti

TEACHERS INSURANCE AND ANNUITY ASSOCIATION
COLLEGE RETIREMENT EQUITIES FUND

Published by
Educational Research
Teachers Insurance and Annuity Association
College Retirement Equities Fund
730 Third Avenue
New York, N.Y. 10017

Library of Congress Cataloging in Publications Data

Milletti, Mario A.
    Voices of Experience

1. Educators— United States— Retirement— Case studies. 2. School
employees— United States— Retirement— Case studies. 3. Retirement—
United States— Planning— Case studies. 4. Retirement— United
States— Finance— Case studies. 5. Teachers Insurance and Annuity
Association. 6. College Retirement Equities Fund   I. Title.

LB2842.2.M54   1984   306'.38   84-15746
ISBN 0-9613704-0-8

Voices of Experience is dedicated to Mark H. Ingraham, who died in 1982 at the age of 86. Dr. Ingraham had a distinquished career of nearly 50 years as a mathematician and dean, almost entirely at the University of Wisconsin. Dr. Ingraham also had a special relationship with TIAA-CREF that spanned several decades and that included writing three books in conjunction with TIAA-CREF that drew on his extensive knowledge of staff benefits and of the retirement experience. The last of these books, *My Purpose Holds*, published in 1974, is an insightful, warm, literate essay about retirement. It is the inspiration for *Voices of Experience.*

"I wonder whether anyone will read these wordy answers . . ."

—76-year-old single woman

"I hope your report can urge others to get busy and do something."

—69-year-old married man

FOREWORD

Voices of Experience offers a realistic, often provocative account of retired life from the personal perspectives of retirees in the TIAA-CREF retirement system.

This book is based on written statements from TIAA-CREF annuitants in which they describe retirement as they have experienced it. Their statements were obtained as part of a comprehensive survey of our retirees conducted in the fall of 1982. Over 1,500 individuals gave us their comments and observations on retirement, many expressing their views with remarkable candor and some writing long essays. We are most grateful to all of them for their valuable contributions.

Mario Milletti of our Educational Research unit has done a superb job of blending these statements with a thoughtful, sensitive narrative. He has crafted a very informative and readable book.

Voices of Experience covers a broad range of retirement considerations, from typical concerns, such as finances, health, and housing, to often unaddressed concerns, such as adjustment difficulties, altered relationship with spouse, and retirement as a single person. We believe the collective wisdom expressed in this book will be extremely useful to our participants looking ahead to their retirement.

TIAA-CREF is publishing *Voices of Experience* as part of our expanded retirement counseling services. Our major interest, as always, is the financial aspect of retirement; we were founded in 1918 to provide annuity income for retired educators and that remains our primary mission. Still, we appreciate that a satisfying retirement involves more than financial security, and *Voices of Experience* reflects our efforts to keep TIAA-CREF participants informed about the multiple factors that shape life in retirement.

It is a pleasure to offer this unusual and, we feel, worthwhile retirement planning guide. We are especially indebted to the "voices of experience"— the hundreds of TIAA-CREF annuitants whose eloquent quotations are the basis of this book.

William T. Slater
Senior Vice President
TIAA-CREF

New York, N.Y.
August, 1984

ACKNOWLEDGEMENTS

Voices of Experience is the result of the contributions of many TIAA-CREF staff members.

I am particularly indebted to Bruce Chapin who labored long and hard with me on this project. Bruce helped categorize and analyze the mountain of comments furnished by our retired annuitants, upon which this book is based. There were literally thousands of separate quotations. In addition, Bruce assisted in organizing the book, wrote early drafts of some chapter sections, and provided editorial suggestions.

Stuart Whalen was the project's statistical expert and guided me through the intricacies of statistical analysis; he was especially helpful in detecting— and sometimes rejecting— subtle relationships and distinctions. In addition, Kathleen Kelleher, Mike Prehoda, Timothy Scerba, Sarah Tobin, and Joan Watson provided assistance at critical junctures.

Betty Meyers had, perhaps, the most difficult role— deciphering and interpreting our annuitants' comments. This was not an easy task since all but a few of them were handwritten. Peggy Eberhart and Jeanette Pitts ably assisted her.

Special acknowledgement goes to my two editors, Steven Weisbart and James Mulanaphy. In addition to being thoughtful, skillful editors, they provided much-appreciated moral support. Jim designed and directed the survey that provided all the raw material for this book and has written *Lessons on Retirement,* a separate statistical report of the findings.

TABLE OF CONTENTS

Chapter 1: THE PURPOSE OF THIS BOOK

This is a book about the personal retirement experiences of TIAA-CREF annuitants. It presents the suggestions and observations of the already-retired for the benefit of the retired-to-be because most of us learn best from experience — our own and others'. Our hope is that by sharing the views of retirement expressed by retirees — these "voices of experience" — we will enable future retirees to plan better for the significant life-change that retirement is. We want to help participants in the TIAA-CREF pension system, and others, prepare for the best of retirement while increasing the chances of avoiding its pitfalls.

The comments that are at the core of this book are based on the replies to two questions that were part of a broad retirement survey we conducted in the autumn of 1982 among TIAA-CREF annuitants. The comments were elicited at the end of a 20-page questionnaire in which we asked our annuitants about their finances, health, housing, activities, retirement preparation, and general satisfaction with retirement. We capped the questionnaire with these open-ended queries: "What are the main attractions and also the main drawbacks of retirement from your point of view?" and "What would you do (or have done differently) to make your retirement more rewarding?"

The response to our survey was exceptional. Of the 2,200 randomly selected people in the survey group, almost 85% returned the questionnaires — sometimes in the face of substantial obstacles, such as a 75-year-old who apologized for mailing her response late because she was recuperating from brain surgery. Summarizing the findings of all the questions in a very general way: most of our retirees are financially well off, in comparatively good health, and well-satisfied with retirement. Understandably, some are worried about inflation, about failing health, and about the high cost of a prolonged illness. While some of our retirees chose not to answer all of the questions we asked, slightly over 1,500 did answer the open-ended questions that are the basis for this book.

Some of the topics that our annuitants write about are common to all TIAA-CREF retirees, while others, because the retirement experience is unique to each of us, are highly individualistic. The surveyed retirees shared their experiences with us willingly and, often, with surprising frankness. One reason for this is that the survey was designed and administered to assure anonymity; we have no way of identifying individuals who replied.

There are, of course, some limitations in relying on volunteered comments as a way for readers to sample retirement: some aspects of retirement are not discussed in detail, or at all, simply because our retirees have not chosen to write much about them. Also, the retirees quoted in this book focus on aspects of retirement that are personally important and, therefore, perhaps overlook matters that would be important to others. Similarly, although our retirees were asked to report their feelings about retirement's advantages as well as its disadvantages, they sometimes exhibit the all-too-human trait of emphasizing what bothers them and ignoring what does not. These limitations are far outweighed by the wealth of useful information our retirees provide. They present a detailed, comprehensive look at the retirement experience from the perspective of true retirement experts— people who are retired.

As readers will notice, our "experts" (like experts generally) don't always agree. Their volunteered remarks clearly show many different and sometimes contradictory dimensions to retirement. That there are contrasting views should be expected, considering the diversity of backgrounds that our survey tapped: the respondents' ages range from 60 to 95, and the group includes faculty, administrators, professional staff, and support staff— just about all the occupations in academe, as shown in the charts on the following page. In addition, some people have been retired for many years; others for only a few. Some are affluent; a few are poor. Most say they are in good health compared to their peers; some are troubled by age-related infirmities.

CURRENT AGE OF THE RETIREES WE SURVEYED

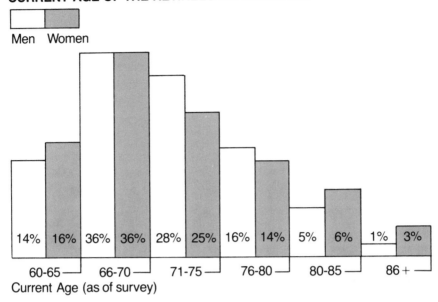

Men Women

| 14% | 16% | 36% | 36% | 28% | 25% | 16% | 14% | 5% | 6% | 1% | 3% |

60-65 —— 66-70 —— 71-75 —— 76-80 —— 80-85 —— 86 +

Current Age (as of survey)

MAIN OCCUPATION DURING THE WORKING YEARS

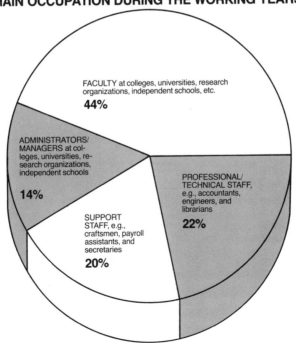

FACULTY at colleges, universities, research organizations, independent schools, etc.
44%

ADMINISTRATORS/ MANAGERS at colleges, universities, research organizations, independent schools
14%

SUPPORT STAFF, e.g., craftsmen, payroll assistants, and secretaries
20%

PROFESSIONAL/ TECHNICAL STAFF, e.g., accountants, engineers, and librarians
22%

In preparing this book, we sifted through thousands of separate remarks. Clearly, we couldn't include all of them, and perhaps some bias crept into our selection process— the eloquent statement favored over the wooden phrase, for example. Sometimes a comment was selected because it underscores an important point, even though that point might have been made only once or twice; sometimes a single comment represents dozens of others in which a single point was repeated over and over again. We have tried to represent fairly what our respondents have to say about the retirement experience by striking a balance between reporting broad insights and highly personal statements, and between bareboned answers and elaborate ones. While we believe that many of the points made in the quotations in this volume apply to retired people in general, readers should remember that because of the occupational backgrounds of our retirees— most worked in education for the major part of their careers— some of their interests, viewpoints, and perceptions may differ from those of the general U.S. retired population.

To provide readers with as many glimpses as possible into the retirement experience, we include in most chapters one or more *Comments* sections, consisting of groups of pertinent quotations. Some chapters contain longer comments, labeled *Essays*, that treat one or more themes so comprehensively or expressively that they are presented pretty much in their entirety. Also, for additional perspective against which readers may consider the views quoted here, we include some statistical data and conclusions developed from analysis of the answers to the survey's other questions. And we present in the final chapter a copy of the survey questionnaire along with the results. Taken together, we hope that the comments in this book— the "voices of experience"— can be a valuable resource to anyone who is thinking ahead to retirement.

Chapter 2: GETTING READY

"If I Had Known . . ."

There is no one "correct" way to approach the retirement experience— the many different points of view in this volume attest to that — but there are points that almost all of our retirees agree on. One of them is to avoid drifting into retirement without preparation. Indeed, our retirees indicate that retirement planning is an important ingredient in retirement satisfaction. They say that planning is helpful because retirement— while a natural outgrowth of our working careers and, indeed, all our previous life— will probably be a new and very different experience.

"If one has not planned for retirement and prepared one's self, it can be devastating. Particularly for those who have only one interest in life— their job," says a 71-year-old man. Adds a 70-year-old man: "I would have done more planning. This would include retirement counseling; I would urge our college to provide this. We need to plan priorities in our mature years. We need to learn how to take risks in learning new careers, new travel skills, new ways to volunteer, and new ways to exercise for health's sake. It would help to plan more for long range health care— and even for losing a spouse."

Another important reason for planning is that the retirement years can represent a major portion of our lives. A 66-year-old man, for example, points out that retirement is "a second life in some respects. After all, one may be retired 10 years, perhaps 15 or 20, maybe even 30 years— that's a lot of days of new living." Adds a 72-year-old man, "Don't get preoccupied with thoughts of old age— you at 70 may have 15 years yet before you are old. Even then you can take on the problems with the same spirit of challenge you have had before."

Retirement finances, our retirees feel, is an area that especially requires attention during the working years. "To be perfectly frank, it never occurred to me in any real sense that one day I would be old," says a 66-year-old woman. "My financial planning was, therefore, very haphazard. My present and future would be less flawed with uncertainty if my financial situation were stronger."

Some retirees suggest developing a budget for the quite different pattern of household expenses encountered in retirement compared to the working years. Others mention, at the very least, anticipating major expenses that might better be made before or early in retirement, such as the purchase of a new car or home repairs. On the income side of the retirement financial equation, retirees stress the need to plan well ahead of time for as adequate level of retirement income as possible. As a 72-year-old man recalls:

"Over too many years my philosophy was: 'consider the birds and the flowers — they store not.' On leaving college I decided to follow nonprofit institution jobs (to be a do-gooder) until I was 40 years of age and from then on make some money — enough to retire on. It didn't quite work out that way. The nonprofit institutions I worked for did not have retirement programs. I was not covered until age 55 when I started a TIAA-CREF program in my private school — a bit late. I would (the next time around) begin on a retirement program soon after entering the work force. Fortunately, things worked out for me, but it could very well have been the opposite. I gambled and made out, but would not do it again or advise others to follow that course."

As described more fully in later chapters, many retirees stress the need to build up personal savings in addition to income from pensions and Social Security — difficult as saving is for so many of us. A 69-year-old man, for example, suggests that "people should be constantly reminded to prepare for retirement, especially from age 45 up, and save a little more than they think is enough." The comments from our retirees suggest that, in addition to providing the financial means to take advantage of retirement's possibilities, additional personal savings helps widen the lifestyle options in retirement and provide flexibility to meet the unexpected. As a 70-year-old widow writes, where we asked what she would do differently if she had the chance, "Although

I have an adequate income, I would plan to save even more for the retirement years."

There are many other aspects of retirement to think about ahead of time, our retirees' comments suggest, and these are also discussed in later chapters. Among them: How to spend spare time in retirement — traveling? with hobbies? in volunteer or part-time work? Should hobbies or interests be developed before retirement? Should work-related activities be continued into retirement, and if they are, would the equipment, secretarial help, office space, and other resources we take for granted during the working years be available? How disciplined are you without the structure of daily work? Will you miss the institutional supports, power, and perks of your job? If married and both spouses work, should both husband and wife retire at the same time? Where will you live? If you want to relocate, when should you start looking for a new home and where do you get solid information about an area? And if you relocate, might you be able to make new — and stimulating — friends? Will you miss old friends and relatives? If you move to a year-round comfortable climate, will you miss the variety of the seasons? Is your health insurance adequate?

As a 70-year-old man observes: "More careful planning during the years immediately prior to retirement would have made retirement more rewarding. Whether to sell one's home, to move to a different region, to rent or buy a new smaller house should be considered carefully. Also figuring out new objectives. Weighing the pros and cons of these and determining a future course of action should all be given due and careful consideration. By so doing, an easier and better transition can be made from the working years to those of a rewarding retirement." According to a 66-year-old widow, "Knowledge is a plus. Explore any avenues which appeal to you — explore fully. Then you are in a position to make wise informed choices when the time comes to make a commitment." A 78-year-old man suggests that potential retirees "begin planning about 20 years ahead of your retirement date. Attend, if possible, courses and programs covering retirement options, and problems as well as suggestions about various plans. Discuss retirement with others in the same age bracket.

Involve your wife in various options, with an added stress on the financial. Visit sections of country to see first-hand retirement potential." Adds a 65-year-old man, "I would have talked with others in retirement before retiring myself. Thus, I might have entered my new life with fewer myths about it."

ESSAY: "WITH PROPER PLANNING, ATTRACTIONS OVERSHADOW DRAWBACKS . . . "

What retirement means to anyone depends on the planning or lack of planning made by the individual concerned.

Saving a portion of income as one goes through life, even if it means some individual or family sacrifices, makes it possible to have more income later in life, such as dividends, interest, and annuity payments above and beyond pensions. For example, I was an officer in the Army Reserve after my active military duty ended following World War II. I devoted time and effort to the Army Reserve program, and this required night work and weekend work that I might have devoted to my family and hobbies. Today my Army retirement check is larger than my Social Security check.

Planning also involves the development of avocational interests. Some people become workaholics. Their vocation is their one and only interest. They seem to think they are indispensable. Yet when they depart from this earth, they are not missed particularly.

The main attraction of retirement is fulfillment. One draw-back may be that you may receive a little less recognition than you received earlier, but really I don't feel that way. That need was met a long time ago. Another drawback of retirement could be that once you reach retirement age you will feel some physical deterioration. With proper planning, I find that the attractions so overshadow the drawbacks that the drawbacks become minimal.

—72-year-old married man

Planning can do much to make activities in the retirement years fulfilling. "If I had known I would live as long as I have, I would have planned a career of accomplishment suited to my retirement years," says an 87-year-old man. "Therefore my advice to anyone beginning a life of retirement is to assume that a long future extends before him and make plans to continue worthwhile creative work." A 68-year-old woman writes that, "You have to structure your new life to replace the gratification that working brought" even though "it often is difficult to find new activities which are all-absorbing." A 72-year-old widow puts it this way: "Retirement is most rewarding when you have tried to prepare for it. You should stay active and communicate with friends and relatives, make friends, etc. Just sitting rocking, having no hobby, staying shut in is quite a drawback. One is just sitting, staring into space . . . "

Another woman, also 72, notes, "Before I retired, I thought lack of duties would be pleasant. I now realize that I should have planned other regular activities." At the very least, during the working years one ought to think about possible hobbies for retirement, the retirees suggest. Says a 63-year-old man who retired early, "I should have acquired a challenging hobby along the way." And a 67-year-old woman writes, "Upon retirement, a person should be sure to have established hobbies and activities. Waiting until retirement to plan these things just doesn't work." A 72-year-old woman's comment that "I would have 'found' a hobby" is echoed by a 66-year-old man's, "We think it is important to somehow inform those who retire to create a hobby."

To get the most out of planning in the case of married couples, both spouses should be involved, our retirees say. A 74-year-old man, for example, writes how: "In retirement, one can pace himself better. This is important since as I get older I find I do intellectual work, such as writing, much better in the morning. But one unexpected disadvantage has been the loss of a quiet work place to think and write. My wife has five TV sets around the house and usually two are going. I would have begun house hunting or planning a year before retirement to assure myself of a home with a quiet office. I ended up with a desk in the basement which is not quiet, comfortable, or attractive. Such planning would have required very much more cooperation by my wife. Some counseling of wives about the changes in retirement would be helpful several years before the date (if it would be accepted)."

Admittedly, a small minority of the retirees seem to favor no planning at all. "While employed I frequently read and heard of the advisability of preparing for retirement, but was too busy to devote any attention to doing so," says a 68-year-old woman. "I now believe that there is over-emphasis on this aspect of retirement." Another 68-year woman agrees, at least as far as the nonfinancial aspects of retirement planning are concerned: "I should think it a mistake to stress 'preparation' for retirement, relocation, activity resolutions, as much as propaganda stresses. Flexibility will win over planning most of the time. 'Setting goals' is only for those who have had the luxury of doing so before retiring. Failing 'goals' might be traumatic. An attitude of *carpe diem* — enjoying the pleasures of the moment without concern for the future— will meet the need of living toward the undeterminable and inevitable which is in store for everyone."

But few disparaged planning. Even the just-quoted woman, despite her belittling of nonfinancial planning, adds, "I should think that care in exploring options for financial security ranks high." The great majority of our retirees favor trying to anticipate in some way their needs in retirement — even though, given life's uncertainties, no one can do so perfectly. Says a 66-year-old woman, who says she is already enjoying retirement while her husband is soon to retire: "So far, we believe we are headed in the right direction for a lifestyle that will be rewarding for us— houses in order, books and tools of the hobbies at hand, concern not to set our expectations too high. We laughingly agreed several years ago that as little signs of diminished capability occur (I, for instance, can't put breakfast onto the table without forgetting at least one item) we would 'be kind to each other and help each other out.' So far that point of view seems to be working splendidly. If disaster strikes it will simply have to be dealt with in whatever way seems best— just as would have been the case if disaster had struck at age 35."

A 73-year-old woman sums up many of the ideas in this chapter: "When no preparation has been made financially or emotionally to live a satisfying life beyond the duration of the job, this creates dissatisfaction. Often, retirement is met as if the person has not been aware of the inevitability of reaching this point. Retirement seems to be accepted with as little preparation as is often present at the death of a loved one or even oneself. When financial arrangements have not or could not, for some reason, be made for retirement, then retirement is truly a drawback. Equally as important is emotional preparation, which includes engagement in satisfying activities."

COMMENTS: PLANNING

Most important. Life planning for retirement with specific interests in:

Hobbies — a variety in which both body and mind may be involved. Hands should be trained to do rewarding physical activities to give a feeling of accomplishment, relaxation, and worthy use of leisure time.

Reading — Subscription to periodicals of special interest and library contacts for free reading, secondary research, and recreation. There is no substitute for a contented mind.

Community Service — Everyone can be of use in the community, whether it be civic affairs, aid to senior citizens, rest homes, convalescents, etc.

It is a personal sin to sit around bored.

—83-year-old single woman

I should have more realistically anticipated retirement problems: financial, aging, lifestyle.

—71-year-old married man

I would have sought information on preparing for retirement, such as information on money management, the pros and cons as to selling my house, and living in a different locality. I would have tried one of those travel tours to experience the good and bad aspects of it and to know how expensive such travel is, and also investigated the recreational possibilities for senior citizens and the civic activities possible. I can still do these things but don't have quite the courage to risk the chances of failure that I would have had when I had a stable job to return to. Now I must proceed more cautiously.

—67-year-old widower

In my case it would have been useful to have considered more than I did the following while I was still actively working:

(1) The matter of possibly relocating after retirement.

(2) Medical and health coverage to supplement Medicare.

(3) A program of physical activities which could be expanded after retirement. In short, health maintenance measures.

(4) More thought as to areas of interest and pursuits to be followed after retirement. A start should be made during the working years.

The last two are a way of saying one should not become so absorbed in one's work as to exclude other things. It probably would make one better at one's work, apart from considerations of a better retirement.

— 67-year-old married man

Planning earlier for retirement would have been wise. Waiting too long has caused a loss of friends who, taking early retirement, moved away in all directions.

— 74-year-old married man

If I could go back to pre-retirement, I would plan more carefully for the after-retirement period by:

(1) Taking a course in retirement which my university offered, or get into a retirement counseling program.

(2) Studying earlier and more thoroughly the financial aspects of retirement.

(3) Plan to continue to work part-time (preferably in a new field) and gradually ease toward total retirement.

(4) Take up more hobbies.

(5) Become involved more with people outside my work situation.

— 70-year-old single woman

My suggestions to those who are not yet retired would be:

(1) Start planning immediately for it. The younger the age the better. Retirement days come sooner than you presently realize.

(2) Obtain membership in American Association of Retired Persons and other such groups, get their materials and books, and begin at least to make tentative plans for your retirement.

(3) Set up an IRA account and and put some amount into it regularly. Also set up other long-range investment programs as can be afforded.

(4) Try to determine what your needs will be by the time you are to retire.

— 69-year-old married man

Formulating specific plans before retirement that will set in motion professional work after retirement can be very important. I have seen this work effectively in my husband's case. After extended work in an entirely different field, he proposed to return to continue earlier work in American Indian

languages. While he was still employed he made plans and secured funding for a brief field visit to reestablish field work connections and has proceeded to fuller funding and work in this area, with a schedule that will take at least five years more to complete. I also made some general preparation for professional work in retirement through a post-doctoral fellowship in a related field.
— *69-year-old married woman*

I'm glad for several things I did do: reading about retirement in popular magazines and books; studying materials and information booklets sent by spouse's pension fund; and talking to friends who were in retirement. We began all of these activities 10 years before actual retirement time.
— *67-year-old married woman*

I should have planned to improve my golf before getting mixed up with my retired friends.
— *80-year-old married man*

I would have actually and consciously enumerated, on paper, how, where, and what outside activities could be incorporated into daily activity to make a smoother transition from working to non-working status. I would have started some of these activities before actual retirement.
— *67-year-old married woman*

I would be more selective of things around me. A few really good things. I would make time for myself so that I would not have been so tired when I did retire. I would have a time plan — plan things to do at different times, such as go on a certain tour in one year, a different one another year. I would have a better plan for investing money.
— *80-year-old single woman*

The main thing I would have done differently would have been to budget more vigorously the time I spent on university committee work and administrative work in the five or ten years before retirement. In retrospect I think I would have been a more effective teacher and researcher in my last years of full-time teaching and a more effective researcher in the first years of retirement if I had begun more systematically to disengage from the tasks of collective management.
— *70-year-old married man*

I feel that it is certainly more stimulating to have *something* to plan toward for at least one or two days each week, be it part-time employment or volunteer projects. This would present a challenge of sorts, and at the same time bring more outside interests into home life.
— *73-year-old married woman*

I should have involved myself more in community activities and participated more in other organizations to which I have belonged for years and still do. Now too old to change.

—84-year-old widow

I would urge everyone to look into hobbies and study or develop them, even if it's looking up your family tree — a lot of history can be acquired in such a pursuit.

—66-year-old married woman

Planning for retirement is not something to be done during the last few years. It must be done all during life. All talents must be developed so that you have more than one interest. Money must be invested wisely and set aside for retirement, all during the working years. If you have done these things, there will be little or no drawbacks to retirement. It is also wise to secure a retirement home (one you have planned or built) about 15 years before retirement.

—82-year-old single woman

Getting Help From Employers

As the preceding pages indicate, our retirees believe that planning can increase the chances of having a satisfying retirement. Many retirees express interest in an obvious source of pre-retirement counseling — employers. "I wish I'd received the counseling some of the young and middle aged are receiving today," says a 73-year-old man. "It is so difficult to impress upon the young how fast you grow old. How do the Pennsylvania Dutch say it— too late smart?"

According to the findings of our survey, such counseling was far from a common practice among the nation's educational institutions. Only about a fifth of the retirees recall that their last employer offered any counseling or other assistance in planning for retirement. However, younger retirees are somewhat more likely than their older counterparts to recall receiving assistance, suggesting that educational employers have been increasing pre-retirement counseling programs for their staff members in recent years. (TIAA-CREF-sponsored retirement planning seminars are described briefly in the following box.)

INCIDENTALLY: TIAA-CREF'S RETIREMENT PLANNING SEMINARS

TIAA-CREF has been conducting seminars throughout the country for participants age 55 and over since 1980. These popular seminars give participants and their spouses first-hand details about their TIAA-CREF retirement benefits and income options. The seminars are run both on a community-wide basis, with invitations sent directly to all TIAA-CREF participants living in the designated area, or for participants employed at a single institution as part of the school's own pre-retirement planning program. During the first four years in which they have been held, over 30,000 participants and their spouses have attended TIAA-CREF's retirement planning seminars.

Pre-retirement planning assistance just before retirement is better than none, but may not be enough, some retirees suggest; the planning help should preferably be available well ahead of time. "It would have been useful if I had begun to consider the matter of retirement much earlier, at least to recognize that there is a life after academia! This would have made the transition easier," says a 67-year-old man. "This consideration should actually begin some years before retirement. A program of retirement preparation counseling just before actual retirement is of limited value."

One 68-year-old, who took a job after he retired, will apparently get the chance to take advantage of what he's learned about the desirability of planning help. "I wish I had some help before my first retirement in terms of personal planning, money, travel, opportunities, etc. I had to learn all the hard way," he says. "I am looking forward to retiring *again* at age 70 — but before I do I will get professional counseling."

COMMENTS: ON PRE-RETIREMENT COUNSELING

Would like to have had more *individual* help on what to do with funds. Also more readily available reliable help. I didn't know where to turn for advice. Much retirement information is based on married couples. The situation of single people is likely to be different.

— 71-year-old single woman

I wish that my last employer had offered an employee counseling service along with their pension plan. It would have helped me understand that I was getting sharply reduced benefits in the health insurance plan I bought when I retired. Retirement without a health insurance medical/surgical plan that is affordable can be a disaster. To lose such a plan is criminal, through no fault of your own.

— 64-year-old married man

My school was too small to have an employee counseling service and planning help. I would have welcomed such a service.

— 66-year-old married woman

The major factors that I would encourage:
   (a) Provide financial guidance seminars to individuals biannually from age 35 years onward. Too many of us are ignorant, and to begin thinking about finances at age 55 is too late.
   (b) Provide health guidance seminars to individuals biannually from age 45 onwards in an attempt to forestall heart attacks, etc.
   (c) Provide "how to use retirement time" seminars to individuals biannually from age 55 onwards — an age near enough (but not too distant) from the retirement age. Some need this guidance.

— 67-year-old married man

Sometime during my first year of retirement, I felt that I was no longer a contributing person in society. I actually felt very unimportant and not needed in society. After being retired for one year, I took an eight session workshop on preparing for retirement. I wish I had that workshop two or three years before retirement. We need to be financially prepared long before retirement, and psychologically we certainly need help. This was my most difficult part. Perhaps I think I should set some long-term goals for my retirement as well as short-term goals. I don't want my years to slip by without some worthwhile changes in my life. Actually, I feel very fortunate that I am retiring now— much is being done to provide good alternatives for senior citizens. One's life certainly can be enriched with some planning and taking advantage of what society offers. I certainly feel that more planning must be done for retirement. Attitude towards retirement is *so* important!

—68-year-old single woman

ESSAY: SOME NEED COUNSELING, OTHERS DON'T

People with few personal resources—serious hobbies, interests, responsibilities, children and grandchildren, the desire to travel — are often understandably apprehensive about pending retirement. But we have seen many far more concerned about the "break" than they should be.

Most of the people we know are busy and as interested as ever. I should think the retirees TIAA is concerned with, for example, would generally need less counseling, say, than retirees from industry. As with everything in life, it is what one brings to an endeavor that is the measure of success. Certainly, education and interests—real cultivated interests — are the key to a rewarding retirement. Then if one has one's health — and we are held back from a rewarding retirement only by health problems—there are virtually no limits. Obviously these things are the result of a lifetime of experience and can hardly be created in a year or so before retirement.

The people who need counseling, it seems to us, are those who fear that the sudden taking away of a formal day-to-day structure will throw their lives into chaos. This is a real dread for some, and they are the ones who need to be encouraged and urged to broaden their own resourcefulness to shape their lives after retirement.

For the rest of us, and there are many I think, though we are grateful for all offers of counseling, the big question at retirement is, "What do I do first? Where do we begin?"

—64-year-old married man

Chapter 3: WHY THEY RETIRED

"I Was Ready For A Change"

Two-thirds of our annuitants say they retired at a time they chose — checking off questionnaire answer options such as "I wanted more time for myself," "I wanted to do other things besides work," or, simply, "I felt it was time to retire." Most of the persons in the retired-by-choice group were clearly attracted to retirement as an alternative to their jobs, and they are the subject of this section.

Compared to the other retirees, a higher proportion of these people believe they had made very thorough — and, in retrospect, very satisfactory — retirement plans; a higher proportion also rate themselves as very satisfied with retirement. Even though members of the retired-by-choice and clearly-attracted-to-retirement group picked their own retirement date, the circumstances surrounding their freedom and ability to choose often differed. Many had a wide-ranging choice of potential retirement dates while others, because of illness or other factors, seem to have had a much narrower range of choices.

An 80-year-old woman explains what attracted her to retirement. She writes, "I helped make the world go around for 45 years and enjoyed it and was ready at age 66 to let someone else have the opportunity." In a similar vein, a 75-year-old man writes: "For 23 years I was in top-level college administration. I strongly believe that at 65 a person should definitely step down. Retirement years start a new phase in life — time for writing, traveling, and doing things where there was no time before. My only wish is that there were more time to do all of the things that need attention, such as more writing and more time for participation in community activities. In fact I really don't feel I have retired. I've just shifted gears and move at a slightly slower pace, enjoying it along the way." Says a 66-year-old woman, who retired at age 64: "The main attractions of retirement are the relief from responsibilities and the opportunity to spend time on what I want to do when I want to do it. I am relieved from the responsibilities of answering the phone, making arrangements, of handing out unpleasant decisions, dealing with parents, of interceding with faculty for students, and so forth. I found my work very interesting but I was ready for a change."

Interestingly, a 73-year-old former librarian uses language similar to the just-mentioned retiree's but cites a different reason — related to health— for retiring at a time of her own choosing, at age 65. She writes: "I worked for 39 years, 4 months and while I was doing the only work I wanted to do, I was ready for a change. I had some health problems and was on sick leave quite often. I looked forward to having time to do the things I had not had the time and energy to do while working. I still have health problems, but I don't have to be concerned about my work now." A 71-year-old man also retired for health reasons — his wife's. "If my wife had had good health I might have waited another few years before hanging up my glove," he says. "As it was, however, I'm sure I made the best choice." And a 66-year-old former economics professor tells how his "last five years of work were my most rewarding and enjoyable— I was a successful teacher respected by my students. Aware of some slackening in energy and powers, I wanted to quit while ahead and to try a different style of life while still energetic enough to do so."

Some were drawn by special interests to retire early, such as a 69-year-old man who retired at age 60. He writes, "I thoroughly enjoyed my career but I wanted more time and the freedom to pursue my interest in traditional Chinese thought without all the ancillary duties and responsibilities imposed by an institution — committees, chairmanship, paper-grading, etc." An 81-year-old man also retired early, at age 63, for matters related to the spirit. In his case, he says his very high income level allowed him to retire early to be his religious denomination's observer at Vatican Council II.

A 71-year-old man left full-time work relatively early, at age 63, with more earthly motives in mind. He describes how he wanted to pursue his avocations: "I had taught for nearly 40 years and decided that I could forego the daily routine and the night duties of boarding school life. Our school is located near a resort where I had been a tennis pro in the summers during my teaching career. I have continued to play golf and tennis there as well as to string racquets. As a teacher I directed plays, and now I do community plays and act in a new theater in town. I also teach a section of my wife's history class. This and my tennis keep me in contact with some of the students; also, my wife and I have a table in the dining room where I meet other students. I am content."

WHEN THEY RETIRED

AGE AT RETIREMENT BY FORMER OCCUPATION

Former Occupation	Percent Retiring			Total	Average Age
	Before Age 65	At Age 65	After Age 65		
College Faculty	27%	33%	40%	100%	65
College Administration	40%	34%	26%	100%	64
Other Professional/Technical	43%	30%	27%	100%	64
Support Staff	51%	34%	15%	100%	63.5
Independent School Faculty and Administrators	55%	30%	15%	100%	63
All Retirees	39%	33%	28%	100%	64

And a 74-year-old man recalls that: "At the university from which I retired, I had the option of retiring at 65 or continuing to 70. Having seen a number of persons who were relatively healthy and active at 65, and over the hill at 70, I decided to have those 5 years for leisure, golf, etc. Also, a little pencil work indicated that the difference between my retirement income and a continued salary was not sufficient to encourage me to stay on.

I *love* retirement — just naturally lazy I suppose. Anyway, I recommend it." A 73-year-old woman, a former head librarian, writes, "I loved the work and was, I think, good at it. But sometimes, as with many administrators, the year seemed to be 13 months long. By age 62 I decided I could live adequately and quite differently. Both conditions highly desirable by then." And an 82-year-old man explains his decision to retire at age 62, "Although I was enjoying a very attractive group of courses, I felt they were becoming more and more routine, without prospect for change. The adventure was over."

Special situations, at their jobs or in their personal lives, caused other people to retire earlier than expected. A 72-year-old widow, for example, notes that, "I retired early (at age 61) to marry the father of a student, my first and only marriage." And a 67-year-old man who retired at age 63 describes how "a faculty 'reconstruction' in our graduate school made retirement desirable and possible for some top-tenured people like myself. I was fortunate to be able to negotiate a mutually satisfactory retirement plan with the university. They bargained with me in good faith and made it possible to retire two years early without major sacrifice of any expected annuity."

He continues: "I have done some of the writing I had intended and I had a chance to return to the ministry (interim) which gave me the chance to initiate and experience many things I had dealt with theoretically in teaching. The faculty of which I was a member has been thoughtful in recognizing its emeriti members in the life of the university. I miss the stimulation of professional meetings which I cannot afford to attend at my own expense. I also miss faculty contacts (luncheons, conversations, some social life, etc.) but I could doubtless have these things if I wanted to push myself into them. Generally, I am happier with my whole lifestyle now than at any other time in my life. That is because I am fortunate to have an interesting professional life to pursue, and enjoy good health."

Some retirees, while welcoming retirement, were at the same time somewhat apprehensive about the life-switch. A 71-year-old man, for example, recounts how, "I had truly enjoyed my job with its varied and challenging assortment of tasks and

---

INCIDENTALLY: RETIREMENT EARLY AND LATE

About 10% of our retirees retired at age 60 or sooner. They usually left their jobs by choice, although some retired due to factors like ill-health or the need to take care of a relative. Their retirement plans were perhaps facilitated by their overall financial situations, which generally were somewhat better than those of other retirees in our survey.

Another 10% of our retirees retired at age 70 or older. Of these, about half were forced to retire because of mandatory retirement age limits at their institutions. Most of the late retirees, no matter why they retired, would have preferred to continue working and disliked the idea of retirement.

---

had worked with a marvelous group of people (with whom I keep in touch)." But, he continues, "An ever-increasing work-load was taking its toll on my ability to cope with everyday pressures and to approach each day with composure and enjoyment. A sixth sense seemed to be telling me it was time to turn the job over to someone else!" Although he retired at age 65 "with a vague feeling of trepidation" he finds that the decision was a correct one for him: "The principal attraction to retirement is the chance it affords to take up a different life as full and attractive as academic life was, and to do this before you are forced to by failing physical and mental health."

Other people welcomed retirement because it presented them with opportunities that perhaps — in view of family and financial responsibilities and the requirements of a career— they couldn't take advantage of earlier. An 80-year-old man, for example, writes how he retired at 65 because he was offered a five-year appointment as an educational consultant in Southeast Asia. And a 65-year-old man, who is currently involved with consulting and partnership with his wife in "our publishing house," says that he retired at age 62 "to work at several things other than what I'd done all my life professionally. The financial capability came with retirement."

In making their decision to retire, many of our annuitants viewed retirement as a part of life's continuum that, as with other phases of our lives, has its own peculiar joys and frustrations. As a recently retired 69-year-old widow puts it: "Retirement has its own built-in potential. People who don't appreciate that point are missing something very vital. Without criticizing them, I have seen that some of my friends are utterly miserable at this time. Several long for 'yesteryear.' Others actually grieve for lost opportunities and bemoan the very nature of life and living. But retirement is simply another aspect of the human experience." A 78-year-old single woman, who retired at age 60 "to do other things besides work," writes that, "I loved teaching— I tried to put my all into it and I spent time on my work. When I discontinued teaching I felt that I had closed one door and was ready to open another."

According to a 71-year-old married woman, who retired at age 65, "I worked all my life — and enjoyed it — so I could retire. Now I'm enjoying every minute of retirement. Keeping busy in a meaningful way is essential. If one has developed interests before retirement, then retirement is a natural sequence." And a 70-year-old man, who retired as planned at age 65, writes: "Retiring before one's capacities, in the overall sense, begin to diminish seems the decent, ethical thing to do— to make room in the societal employment track for someone else (younger, of course) who's ready and deserves and needs the opportunities you have had. Retirement at about 65 seems to be quite compatible and reasonable within our social structure and with our aspirations for a good quality of life. By age 65 one should have attained most of one's professional goals and expectations, and have time to enjoy— reap— the benefits."

The Mandatorily Retired

One-third of our retirees were not able to completely control their retirement date. Most of this group retired— or perhaps more accurately, were retired — because they reached their employer's mandatory retirement age. Not surprisingly, a smaller percentage of the mandatorily-retired-for-age group say they were looking forward to retirement than was true for other groups. But those retired for age aren't dominated by pessimists about retirement: for every one who says that prior to retirement he (or she) disliked the idea of retiring, there are two who indicated they were actually looking forward to retirement or at least were ambivalent about it.

A 77-year-old scientist, mandatorily retired at 65, writes about his ambivalence. First he notes that he is "reasonably satisfied" with retirement and relieved that "my weekly— Friday — headaches have disappeared and my blood pressure is down to normal for my age." Then he adds a regret: "I can no longer use the scientific and professional expertise I spent 50 years accumulating. I was a recognized expert in certain scientific and professional fields."

A former administrator, now 78 and who was also retired at 65, had been looking forward to retirement even though it was imposed. He explains: "My job at the university involved responsibility for an extensive building program and it involved dealing with the faculty, the deans, the business department, the chancellor, the board of trustees, the city planning commission, state agencies, members of the legislature, federal agencies, and a private donor. To get all these different people to agree on what a building should be was frequently a major task of negotiation. Until shortly before I retired, I found this a fascinating task. However, by the time I reached mandatory retirement age I was just plain tired. I would not have missed the experience for anything, but I had just plain had enough of people-problems and was happy to have time to pursue my own hobbies, which have kept me reasonably busy, happy, and seldom bored ever since." Similarly, a 74-year-old man, who had been involved with medical school administration, writes that he was looking forward to the retirement required by mandatory age rules. "I was tired after nine exhausting but exhilarating years," he writes.

Of our retirees who disliked the idea of retiring due to age restrictions, at least one of them, a 75-year-old former library administrator, did continue to work, although he was not totally happy about the arrangement. He recalls: "My university had an age 65 retirement requirement for administrators. They asked me to stay on for another year to help continue operations while they searched for my successor. At age 72 they called me back as a consultant to assist in various programs, i.e., history of the school, records management, exhibits, and various activities. 'You're the only one that knows enough about it,' they told me, or 'You're the only one that can do this job for us — advise us, etc.' Why couldn't I just continue on the job which I performed with credit? My retirement status: curator emeritus. Modestly, I could have done a better job than my three successors. I'm still there and very much in demand. But at 75, I prefer to have my own time. I enjoy the poetry of each passing hour."

Most of the mandatorily-retired who did not want to retire were not as fortunate as the just-mentioned librarian. Some of them are unhappy because they feel that their valuable skills are not being used. A 74-year-old former nursing educator is an example. "Is 65 such a magic number?" she writes. "You reach it and then your work days are ended. No one considers that a person hasn't changed. One doesn't become incapable overnight. Why can't we continue to serve? Because I dislike retirement so much, I haven't really enjoyed it. There aren't enough challenges." Adds a 78-year-old man who retired at age 70: "We have plenty of skills and vast stores of knowledge that can be of great value in the education of youth. And *experience*, judgement, compassion, and understanding. For example, we can pass on our experience of how chemistry or physics or astronomy has developed during the past half century. We have seen how economic policies that seemed so promising have failed in the long run. We have seen how political policies that seemed to us in our youth to be so good or so bad have actually turned out to be so bad or so good, or really irrelevant."

A similar complaint comes from a 71-year-old former educator in the performing arts, forced to retire because of age at 67, writes: "I think the biggest drawback is retirement before the individual wants to — particularly in the arts, where one is working on a one-to-one basis. Great teachers have taught into their 90s." A 90-year-old man who was opposed to his mandatory retirement — at age 70 — echoes the point: "Some have their best years after a prescribed or mandatory retirement age."

Yet some of the mandatorily-retired who initially opposed retirement, such as the following 77-year-old woman, have found that they indeed enjoy retirement. She says: "As a busy counselor, I felt reluctant to step out of the mainstream; I would have favored retiring at age 68 or 70 rather than mandatory 65. Perhaps others in good health feel that dread. However, those early three or five years provide time to make new friends and to develop new interests. Having accepted the break, I find it's good, too — so long as we can pay our bills." Adds a 76-year-old woman: "I dreaded the thought of retirement as it approached and had made no conscious plan. In fact, I went on a 10-week tour of the Eastern European nations at the time my university opened after I retired so that I would not be around to feel sorry for myself. But now I am a happy, busy retired person. Why? In thinking about what I really enjoy since I have retired, I realize most of my life has been a preparation for the things I enjoy in retirement."

It may well be that changes in the law since most of the surveyed group retired will do much to blunt criticism of age restrictions. According to a 72-year-old man: "When I was forced to retire at 65, I was not ready. I had not planned to retire until I was 70. I am pleased the federal government has raised the mandatory retirement age to 70. At 65 I was not mentally or financially ready to retire; at 70 I was, and did on my own."

A Variety Of Other Retirement Reasons

Within each of the two broad groups of retirees we've mentioned — the two-thirds who retired when they chose and the one-third who couldn't control their retirement date — are people who retired for reasons other than the clear attractions of retirement or because of mandatory age limits. In a few of these cases, their primary stated reason for retiring was straight-forward; the retiree either retired by choice or not by choice. In many of these situations, however, the stated reasons for retire-ment involve a complex of elements that are often difficult to disentangle.

The simpler-to-decipher category includes people who say they were forced into retirement because of loss of government grant funds, or who had to retire because of family responsibili-ties, such as caring for an invalid parent, or because a spouse was transferred. Some were simply unhappy with their work situa-tions and a number say their retirement was triggered by employer cutbacks.

The latter examples include a 74-year-old who had to retire at age 71 because of "the financial condition of my private school." He writes that, "I was left hanging in the air with many unfinished projects. I feel anyone in excellent health and doing an outstanding performance should never be forced to retire. Forced retirement presents emotional and psychological prob-lems that are devastating, even affecting the physical health." While this retiree rates himself as "not satisfied with retirement," others who lost their jobs because of factors outside their control view retirement in a more favorable light. For example, another retiree, now 60 and forced to retire at age 55 — "The German Department, which I headed for more than 20 years and had a long tradition at my school, was systematically dismantled by a Germanophobic new headmaster" — rates himself as "reason-ably satisfied" with retirement. A 67-year-old man, forced to retire at age 61 from his research organization — "my job was eliminated" — now says, "The best thing about retirement is that I have my freedom and can spend my time doing what I want to do instead of having to cater to my superiors. I keep busy on all sorts of interesting activities that keep my mind and body functioning. In many respects, this is the most enjoyable time of my life."

Illness of relatives played a role in other retirement deci-sions. A 68-year-old man, who points to several reasons for his voluntary retirement, at age 62, adds, "I wanted to go to the West Coast and spend some time with my ailing mother before she died." A 73-year-old widow, who worked at a private secondary school, explains, "My husband was ill. The school I was working for relocated, requiring a move I did not want to make at that time."

The preceding retiree is one of many whose retirement decision seems to have been a blend of choice and necessity, with the primary motive unclear. With a similar blend of motives, a 62-year-old woman says she retired at age 54 because of a "conflict with the new department chairman" and because "I needed to take over the family farm operation and because of a dependent brother." And in another instance, that of the following 73-year-old, it isn't clear whether he was pushed or pulled into an early retirement from his position as a placement director. While he explains his retirement by checking off questionnaire answer options like "wanted more time for self" and "wanted to do other things besides work" and says he would "retire at same age" if he could do it over again, he also writes the following:

"I was glad to get out of the rat race created by the antiwar demonstrators during the 1960s in higher education. After some 30 years in education, it was a bit more than I could take to have my role as a helper of students changed to that of an enemy simply because I was a college administrator. It made my whole career seem rather useless, or at least pointless. I had started my college teaching career following military service in World War II, and the contrast between the students of the '50s and those of the late '60s was something that most of us did not readily adjust to. I have not regained any feeling or enthusiasm for education since."

Retiring A Little Bit At A Time

Some of our retirees, mostly those who worked in professional capacities, thought that the transition between a working career and retirement could be made smoother. In fact, the word "shock" shows up in several quotes as our retirees describe the abruptness with which retirement seems to have occurred for them. A 66-year-old man puts it this way: "Going from full employment to full retirement in one step seems like the shock a plant must experience when removed from the hothouse to frigid climes." Hence, a frequently mentioned recommendation from this group was that retirement occur in phases. A former chemistry professor for example, observes: "Retirement, like aging, should be a gradual process. It simply does not make sense that an individual can be fully employed and active on any given day and completely retired on the next."

The bridge between full-time work and full-time retirement, retirees suggest, should be part-time work — or is part-time retirement a better phrase? A 66-year-old man, for example, tells how "the two days a week I continue to spend in my profession is making my retirement most rewarding, since it permits me to maintain my job skills and my professional contacts as well as allowing me to grow in my profession and even branch out into related fields. I would strongly recommend to any future retiree that he continue work part-time, either in his profession or a new endeavor, rather than retire totally." A former department chairman, now age 79, wishes that she could have followed such a strategy. "I would like to have had an interval of part-time teaching or research and more travel in the earlier years," she says. "Retiring abruptly at a fixed age is a shock that could be avoided. I wish I had gone somewhere else for a year or two." Adds another former educator, age 87: "I believe that some part-time work after retirement is an advantage. It allows for gradual adjustment from a full work schedule to a limited and then non-remunerative schedule." A former engineer, age 72, offers this specific plan for phased-in retirement: "I believe everyone should have to retire mandatorily at age 45, assume a secondary role until 55, then retire permanently. The good life comes too late in life."

To be sure, partial retirement can have drawbacks, too, according to a 67-year-old. "I still have a few (5 to 8) students but they tend to be marginal compared to the mainstream group (40 to 80) when I was teaching full-time," he writes. "Unfortunately, your colleagues exert their bureaucratic clout and give you the marginal course that nobody wants. And unfortunately, the students become aware of the lack of bureaucratic clout that a part-time retired professor has and they scramble for the most secure base they can find. Total retirement might be better."

While the preceding retirees value partial retirement primarily as a way to retain work ties, others, such as the following, see it as a way to test the waters of retirement without diving in completely. One person who did retire in stages, by leaving full-time teaching for part-time teaching before completely retiring, writes that phased-in retirement "provides a time of emotional acceptance of this stage of life and also an opportunity to establish other relationships not work-connected while testing activities, interests, and hobbies." And a former college administrator points to additional advantages. She writes: "I would have liked the opportunity to take a leave of three to six months to try out retirement before actually doing so. The real experience of being retired cannot be understood fully unless one is able to undergo some sampling of it: a person's real feelings about being severed from the marketplace would then become more clear. If organizations, businesses, and institutions could devise ways of making it possible to take pre-retirement tryout leaves before making a final decision, it would be a boon to the individuals concerned, especially those who are ambivalent about it."

ESSAY: "AVOID THE SHOCK OF ABRUPT CHANGE . . ."

I retired with several particular advantages:

(1) A professional field in which I was able to continue on a part-time basis for 10 years beyond my official retirement — some times for pay and sometimes gratis (National Academy of Science, etc.) — and, even after giving up all formal consultations and other professional activities, a continuing, though lessened, association with my former colleagues and organizations, which keeps me still knowledgeable in my field.

(2) The nature of my consulting and advisory assignments required a great deal of travel (including many trips across

the US and overseas) during which we could combine business with pleasure, since my wife could go with me.

(3) Carrying on, as I did, a variety of interest and activities outside my professional work during my active years (including a consuming hobby), I have been able to continue these extra activities which has greatly eased the giving up of professional work.

(4) A financial situation which permitted us to enjoy these activities and advantages without great worry; our children had received excellent education (college and graduate studies) and are well established and will be able to provide equally good education for their children.

(5) And, finally, a state of health enjoyed by my wife and me that has made our retirement years a source of continuing alertness, both mental and physical, and a sense of well-being and happiness. For our remaining years we now live in a retirement community with full health care facilities and other services provided especially for care of aging people. Our son and family live within convenient driving distance.

I want to conclude with some firm ideas that have come from my experience: Do not wait until retirement approaches to prepare for the change. Live a broad enough life so that you can develop and keep activities and interests outside your main job to carry over into retirement. And if possible, so arrange your career that you can continue part-time in your active field to avoid the shock of abrupt change from one way of life to another completely different one.

—81-year-old married man

Chapter 4: ADAPTING

Getting Used To Retirement

Some of our retirees quickly adapted to retired life, as the following 68-year-old has. "My adjustment, despite lack of preparation, was instantaneous," she writes, "even though I had always found my career most challenging, interesting, and rewarding." But many find that the early period of retired life is one of uncertainty as they undergo a growing realization not only of retirement's attractions (such as independence, leisure, reduced stress) but also of its drawbacks (among them lower income, loss of status, potential for aimlessness). As a 66-year-old woman notes: "No matter how well planned, time is needed to develop a new balance financially, socially, and professionally." Overall, our retirees seem to have adapted quite well: over 90% rate themselves as either "very satisfied" or "reasonably satisfied" with retirement.

Our retirees offer several reasons why the transition from full-time work to full-time retirement may not always be a smooth one. A 75-year-old woman writes: "Any retiree, particularly a female, should face the inevitable fact that circumstances beyond her control, such as one's own health, spouse's health, parents' health, and limited finances, are going to limit her choices of things to do. Choices must be made within those limits." A 64-year-old points to a transitional problem married couples may have: "We have been very happy so far in our one year of retirement. We have been able to do some traveling and have been busy with other activities we both enjoy, but some adjustment had to be made in learning to live together 24 hours a day after years of both working. However, we are making that adjustment satisfactorily." A 60-year-old man describes how "the very real difficulties of professionally letting go and of backing off were never adequately addressed or personally considered. It has not been a missing of the involvement in the office, and only very slightly missing regular contact with former colleagues. Rather, it is the trying to lessen the former drive, the need to contribute, which leads to a subconscious smoldering frustration." An 80-year-old woman adds a related thought: "If you were very active you miss having to be at a certain place at a certain time. You miss the organization of time and activity. Unless you have planned well, you feel at loose ends."

A particularly difficult part of the adjustment process for some retirees is the loss of an institutional role and all that is associated with it. For example, a 71-year-old man, who retired voluntarily at age 62 in order to "give my remaining years to our institute of behavioral studies" writes: "The day before retirement you are somebody, you have the power and respect. The day after you are a has-been. This leads to a psychological shock from which some retired persons never recover. They must be kept professionally busy." If he had it to do over again, he adds, he would retire at an older age. A 75-year-old man, who looked forward to his voluntary retirement at age 67 and would retire at the same age, makes a related point: "A drawback of retirement is loss of clout! After a decade, a university professor does not have the same status!" A 67-year-old woman, who retired at age 63 because she was unhappy in her job and also because her spouse retired then, puts it this way: "There is a sense of almost a loss of identity, especially in the early retirement years. Present activities seem far less important than the activities and duties in the work-a-day world. Consequently personal worth seems diminished. Personal contacts are far fewer in the present, simpler, day-to-day activities." A 66-year-old former dean and provost describes how "one is not involved in campus politics or faculty meetings— though I attend occasionally. Being partially retired is still a loss of authority and status. There is increasing isolation from younger members of the faculty and community both socially and in community groups."

The loss of an institutional setting remains particularly painful for some. Says a 76-year-old woman, who retired from her librarian's job at age 67: "I truly liked my work and devoted my time and thought to it almost exclusively— many overtime hours voluntarily. I believe, along the way, I had the satisfaction of helping younger associates to have a true respect for work. In fact I know that is so — a pride in a well-done job and self respect. That is in the past, of course, and I think I carried it to extremes. Now I can't seem to find the impetus to enrich my life with other interests, an admission hard to make, but an honest one."

A 69-year-old man summarizes many of these feelings: "As I see it, one of the big drawbacks to retirement is the big let-down you feel. You feel left out of the mainstream of things that used to matter a great deal to you. You suddenly realize a loss of ego, of self-esteem. You no longer carry much clout. You are no longer involved in making many decisions. You suddenly find that you are primarily a caretaker of the house and yard, a gardener. Granted, these are fine activities but they are a big let-down from university faculty activities."

Some also miss the atmosphere — intellectual and other-wise — that was part of the job. A 66-year-old woman, for example, comments, "I miss the academic environment in some ways, both the ritual and the friends," while a 67-year-old man wistfully recollects "the close professional friendships and some of the competition." What was important to a 65-year-old woman was "good discussions in my fields of training and experience." A number report becoming increasingly out-of-touch with their chosen field. They include the 66-year-old man who says that the "loss of social contacts with peers" results in "a feeling of being out of the mainstream of daily events in my profession," and the 64-year-old man who laments that "you lose most of the resources to keep up with the profession's advances." There are not-so-obvious let-downs as well, according to a 66-year-old widow: "In the groups I now work with there are clear distinc-tions between those who are working and therefore have Xerox rooms, and secretaries, and drawing accounts, and those who are retired and have trouble even getting a letter typed. As anyone can see by this typing, my working life was spent where there were good secretaries."

People adapt to retirement in various ways. A phased-in retirement, as described in the previous chapter, is one tech-nique. Some, like the following 65-year-old woman, who left her job at age 54 when her husband left his, thought a long trip would be a good way to help prepare for the change from full-time career work to retirement. She writes: "We planned very carefully for my husband's retirement. We had saved for years in order to make a long trip to break the pattern of daily commuting, to remove him from any temptation to check on his successor, and to get away long enough and far enough to get some perspective on our new circumstances and make plans for the future.

"Therefore, we spent two months during the winter of 1980-81 in New Zealand and Australia, spending 10 days with a family in Aukland (fellow English teachers and pen pals). We then flew to Sydney, and after some time there came back across the Pacific by ship to Los Angeles. The ship made stops (brief) in Fiji, Samoa, and Hawaii, but we had plenty of time to talk and plan for the future. For *any* couple, we recommend they break the pattern between work and retirement in some way. A long trip accomplished that purpose for us, and was well worth saving for."

A 69-year-old man recalls how he adjusted, writing: "I do miss the classroom — the lectures and the contacts with students. I always found the classroom and teaching to be great tranquilizers. I miss the social aspect of academia, such as having lunch with colleagues and the congenial association with many of my colleagues during the working day. I am not sure that this is a drawback because the pace is slower. This means that one has to make adjustments in one's lifestyle. This is a problem that many retirees do not or can not solve. I did have a problem in settling down, but with a wide selection of hobbies and activities it was quickly and satisfactorily resolved."

Other retirees seek to make the transition between career work and retirement with volunteer or work (paid and unpaid) activities, as described more fully in a later chapter. A 71-year-old woman, for example, who works part-time for a social agency, says, "My profession was my life. I found I could not tolerate full retirement and after six months I returned to part-time employment. I doubt that I would enjoy full retirement, even with financial security."

Certainly, part-time work or volunteer activities do not always provide the same satisfactions as full-time work, as a 69-year-old widow notes. She says, "With temporary work I never felt completely involved." And a 73-year-old man comments that "the commonly recommended substitute lifestyle of hobbies and volunteer work would be a pretty poor replacement." Part of this dissatisfaction may be that most people approach full-time paid work and volunteer activities with vastly different attitudes, as this 73-year-old woman observes. "Having been accustomed to a highly organized work situation in which productivity was high," she writes, "I discovered that volunteer situations rated low on these points. There was not a sense of achievement."

A 66-year-old man describes his problems with volunteer work, a problem apparently compounded by the loss of institutional-related esteem, and how he adjusted to the situation. He recalls: "A drawback of retirement, I suppose, is the loss of status. I tried working with the local school system but that soon wore thin— they were not on the same frequency of conceptual planning. I would have been in their way. There was no new growth for me and I was worn out trying to convince people they were wrong. I met a high school classmate whom I hadn't seen for 42 years and who lives about five miles away. She introduced me to a commission on aging. It has been a whole new batch of experiences and new learning. Some of the status loss has been won back. I feel like a whole person again."

Working in retirement proved to be particularly successful — and a very pleasant surprise — for another retiree. A 74-year-old man discovered that after "working extremely hard during my career years— seven days a week at least 10 hours per day during the last 20 years— to start two new medical schools, I was afraid that when I retired I would have little to do in my field of competence and experience. To my complete surprise, consultations came quickly. I have been surprised at the difference in making recommendations before and after retirement. After, one can say exactly what he believes is best without worrying about how it reflects on his university; also you do not worry if recommendations are not accepted or acted on."

An 82-year-old, who retired at age 62, was also pleasantly surprised at how he adapted. After describing how one important reason for retiring was to move to "a small holding in New Mexico which I purchased and improved for the happiest years of my life," he writes: "Retirement, in a very real sense, is to renounce a full way of life. So, for success, one should find an equally full mode of life to replace the old. My good fortune was to find the answer to my need in a way of life entirely different from anything I had ever known. I can now look upon my academic life and my 'Western' life both with sobered regret and appreciation. My only point here is that retirement has to be filled with something big and fulfilling— incessant travels, cocktail parties, and such cannot be enough."

However they did it, most retirees seem to have adjusted successfully to whatever might have initially disturbed them about retirement. When the unexpected occurs, though, the transition from work life to retirement life can be particularly difficult. Recalls a former astronomer, whose plans for part-time retirement work in his field suddenly fell apart, "I was dropped into a black hole." A 70-year-old former teacher at an independent school faced a different problem. He recalls: "All my plans for a smooth transition from a busy schedule over to a happy retirement two years hence were exploded by an urgent telephone call to school stating that my wife had collapsed. Immediate retirement was a must! It had been difficult making the change so rapidly and I couldn't get used to retirement as it was an entirely different way of living." But people bounce back. This same retiree adds: "Eight years is a long recovery period but it has been wonderful. It has been so rewarding, as we have been together."

In more-typical circumstances, the length of the adjustment period will vary depending on individual circumstances. "There is some initial feeling of being cast adrift," writes a 68-year-old man. "This feeling soon passes." Remembers a 77-year-old woman, "After the initial year of adjustment to retirement, I've appreciated a relaxed schedule of activity." According to a 63-year-old widower, "My only drawback was the first two years of retirement, of overcoming the feeling of being so non-productive. Now I have learned to love it." Adds a 72-year-old widow, "Retirement is a big adjustment for everyone — we should prepare for that time during our working years. When it does catch up with us it takes at least three years to adjust."

An important element in the adjustment process, our retirees say, is the need to approach retirement with the proper attitude — to appreciate both retirement's pitfalls *and* its potential. As a 79-year-old man writes: "Good retirement life is not just monthly income sufficient to live a reasonably good existence. Half of it — oh, I don't know whether 50/50 or 40/60, or whatever— has got to be *state of mind.*" According to a 63-year-old man, "As long as one is healthy, there's no problem. Obviously, life has more boring periods, less excitement, etc., but nature has a way of coping with these realities. One better learn to *adjust*. There are no real drawbacks; it's part of the life cycle." Says a 66-year-old woman: "I regard this phase of life as yet the next in the sequence we all go through— a time to enjoy what is offered in the way of leisure and freedom from responsibility— not a time to worry about what is impossible (like a return to a girlish figure) or to have regrets about the past."

A 67-year-old woman admits to "a worrisome feeling that one doesn't know for what to prepare. Will income keep pace with costs? Will there be long, expensive illnesses? Must paid help be found one day to do tasks and errands we ourselves do now?" But, she adds, "We can't foresee the future. We can only hope we've done what we could to provide comfort and serenity, and continue a spirit of happy expectation and enthusiasm." And a 65-year-old woman says, "Retirement never meant entry to an idle life. Instead, it was an opportunity to pursue a special interest I had had for many years but couldn't afford to try."

Our retirees offer other advice on how to make the transition from work to retirement. "Don't sit and vegetate," a 78-year-old man urges. "Too many people retire just to grow old." A 75-year-old woman notes, "No retiree can afford self-pity— it's worse than alcoholism or arthritis." And according to a 72-year-old man, "Don't hesitate to try new things. Health permitting, you can do more than ever before. The freedom is real. Take advantage of it."

COMMENTS: SOME THINGS YOU HAVE TO ADJUST TO

Drawbacks: Loss of professional status, identity and contacts
              Loss of daily on-the-job human feedback
              Loss of purpose
              A feeling of second class citizenship
              Loneliness
              Gain in weight
Attractions: More relaxed schedule
              An opportunity to live half of the year in Hawaii
              Time for lengthy trips both throughout the USA and other
                 countries
                                      —*67-year-old single woman*

The main drawback of retirement is being only on the fringes of an exciting, ever changing, and stimulating educational institution.
                                      —*66-year-old single woman*

I'm out of the mainstream of research. Others make the decisions, undertake the planning, direct the endeavor. I probably have the attitude of the old draft horse who doesn't know how to relax and hand over the torch. Nevertheless, there is something missing in somehow being out of the group and advising (at least) on the course to be followed.
                                      —*67-year-old married man*

The sudden change from complete involvement to complete unwinding can be too drastic. For one year I relaxed and did only what I wanted to do when I wanted to do it. I thoroughly enjoyed it but at the end of the year it was hard to "wind myself up" and get back into the swim. Since I am a "people" person I got involved in volunteer work, organizations, boards, committees, etc., but after almost five years of retirement I find that these things do not replace the personal relationships I had in my career years.
                                      —*70-year-old single woman*

Drawbacks: I miss the camaraderie of the university colleagues
              I miss the students with bright, inquiring minds
              I miss the prestige of a university affiliation
              I miss the mental stimulation of working with others on
                 research projects
Attractions: Being able to choose how to spend your time
              Freedom from the parts of my teaching job I did not like,
                 such as grading papers
              Leaving the rat race of campus politics
                                      —*71-year-old married woman*

Both my wife and I expected that as we grew older our physical condition would deteriorate, our financial position might be worse, and we might be unable to indulge in as many activities as we had earlier. As we perceive our situation, we are significantly better off than we expected to be. Hence we feel lucky and hope that our luck holds out for as long as possible, knowing, however, that inevitably it will end.

—71-year-old married man

The stimulation of professional work, the exchange of ideas, and the prestige of identification with a university or medical center— these losses are jolts to one's ego.

—77-year-old single woman

A drawback of retirement is facing the realities of aging. But I am content with our preparation and situation. We are Christians (Quakers) and have made each step of our lives a matter of prayer — seeking God's promised guidance. We are grateful for the reality of His presence. This is true for everyone, that He is there and we can respond, "The Lord is my Shepherd, I shall not want . . . "

—72-year-old married woman

I wouldn't have continued collecting research data for so long — up to retirement. I have an orange crate of data that needs to be analyzed and written up. A retired person's conscience should not be nudged in this way.

—74-year-old married man

Frequently, there is the necessity to move because one must vacate a school-owned apartment or house, or because they must go to a place which is less expensive or otherwise less burdensome. This involves choices about where to live, how to make new friends, how to keep in touch with old friends . . .

—67-year-old married woman

Because of my responsibilities in caring for parents, I did not think of myself as retired until their deaths and my husband's retirement. In retirement, we feel more in control of our lives, activities, and health . . . However, *before* retirement, we both should have disciplined ourselves to do the writing we'd like to do now. Now, we're too busy— or too tired! So far, the only effect of aging that we notice is getting tired sooner.

—65-year-old married woman

One unforeseen drawback upon retirement was a sense of being put on a shelf, or the "end of the road." This feeling was projected from family, co-workers, and others. Happily, this feeling fades away.

—71-year-old married man

ESSAY: "I DIDN'T THINK I'D HAVE ANY DIFFICULTY, BUT . . . "

The only thing I would have done differently to make my retirement more rewarding would have been to start some activity completely different from what I had been doing, and very attractive to me, as soon as possible. Building stone walls, gardening, travel overseas to visit grandchildren —all of these were things that I had done before retirement. Retirement just gave me the opportunity to do more of the same things (with financial limitations on travel). What I needed, and didn't realize I needed, was something that was different. More research and writing in the same old areas turned me off, and I think I had been bored with that for the last five of my 40 to 50 years in academe. I finally found something interesting and exciting but it took me more than a year to find it. That first year was difficult.

A serious drawback of retirement is a lack of firm deadlines. It is all too easy to let something go until tomorrow, and the next day, and the next. I didn't think I had any problems, but my wife says that I did. She says that six months to a year after retirement I became irritable, paced the floor talking, had a nasty temper, and was generally an unpleasant person to have around. Looking back, I think I was bored.

I retired in June, but taught summer school and so I wasn't really retired until August. In October we went to visit a married daughter and some grandchildren overseas. In the following April I was outside building a stone wall and other things, and after a few months and another trip I started sculpture classes and have been very busy ever since. In the months between October and April I had nothing to do, the weather was bad, my wife was at work, and I was bored and frustrated. She thinks I could have developed more problems if I hadn't gotten outside in the spring to build stone walls, lay a stone terrace, get a garden started, *etc., and then started doing sculpture indoors when the weather closed in. Looking back, I think she was probably right.*

I didn't think I would have any difficulty adjusting, but I guess I did. I suggest doing something, especially something new and different, as soon as possible after retiring. Perhaps, if I had started sculpture classes a few months after retiring, there would not have been any problems in that first year. But at that time I didn't know I would enjoy sculpturing so much, and certainly didn't know that I needed to do such a thing.

Fifty years ago I wanted to do sculpture, but as my responsibilities increased I found less and less time for it. About a year after retirement, I signed up for a sculpture class at a local museum school. After getting my hands into it, I began combining my mathematical background with my interest in sculpture, and retirement gave me the freedom to do as I liked with help from a teacher but no pressure to follow a particular style. I calculate and construct mathematical objects. My teachers don't know any mathematics and think I am developing some abstractions, which they like. I try to explain to them what I am doing, and they try to help me. It's not great art, but I'm enjoying it thoroughly. I think every retired person should do something like this, totally different from what they did for so many decades. I can't see why any live person should be bored.

I hope your report can urge others to get busy and do something. The greatest advantage of retirement is the freedom to do what one wants to do, and the related freedom not to do what one does not want to do.

— 69-year-old married man

Chapter 5: FREEDOM!

"I Am Free! Free! Free!"

The most distinctive feature of retirement for our retirees was that, after many years of wishing it were so, their time was now pretty much under their control. "I'm free of responsibilities for the first time since age 12," says a 72-year-old woman. Many were unrestrained in their enthusiasm about their newfound independence, such as the 76-year-old man who writes, "I am free! Free! Free!"

A 69-year-old man describes his newfound freedom this way: "The only limitations on my activities are money and the Ten Commandments." And while a 72-year-old woman enthuses that now "I can take time to smell the roses," a 68-year-old woman writes how she turned fancy into fact: "For years I had wanted to go to Greece, but I wanted to go in the spring when the wildflowers are in bloom — something that isn't possible when you're teaching. So I celebrated my retirement in 1981 by spending the month of April in Greece."

The retirees frequently refer to symbols such as clocks, calendars, schedules, and deadlines to illustrate how time constraints no longer dominate their lives. "No more slavery to clocks and calendars," writes a 70-year-old man. "I've gotten off the schedule treadmill," says a 74-year-old widow. Adds another 74-year-old woman: "After almost 10 years of retirement I still appreciate not having to live by the clock. In all my working years I never used an alarm clock. My inner clock woke me on time. That habit, I have discovered, was very easily broken." To a 75-year-old, "The best feature of retirement is no definite schedule — I threw away my watch the first year. Promptness was almost a disease with me and what a release to be able to go when and where you pleased." An 81-year-old former nurse remembers how she was constantly "on call" for work in the laboratory and surgery and now, "I no longer dread hearing the telephone ring, which 75% of the time meant going back to work day or night for emergency calls." In short, says an 82-year-old woman, "You don't have to hurry, hurry, hurry."

Retirement's freedom brought with it pleasant surprises in the daily routines of our retirees' lives. Retirees write about the advantages of shopping and working out at health spas during off-peak hours, riding public transportation after the rush hour, making doctor appointments more easily, and even having more time to walk the dog. A 69-year-old New Englander writes: "Frankly, one of the main attractions of retirement is that I don't have to drive to the university in a winter storm. There's something relaxing about watching it snow while I have a second cup of coffee."

Another 69-year-old man observes that: "After 50 years it is wonderful to be able to do almost whatever I desire without reference to a schedule — even to taking short trips with my wife on impulse. We can indulge in exercise or recreation of a wide variety, which we could hardly work into our schedule before. I can go on shopping trips — seldom done before. If we start to plan some major event — a long trip, maybe — we can work out the schedule with ease and no conflicts. I enjoy not having to think about the insolvable problems which seem to abound in schools today. Relaxation and regular exercise probably are improving my health." At the same time, a 67-year-old woman says simply, "There's more time to think, to read, to enjoy, to putter, to explore."

Many found the chance to sleep — either later in the morning or uninterruptedly — a treat. "I love doing what I want to do when I want to," says a 63-year-old woman. "I enjoy staying in bed until 6:30 a.m. instead of getting up at 5:15 a.m. when I worked. It is so nice not have to jump when somebody wanted something. I was accustomed to it for 42 years, but life has taken on a new meaning." Adds a 79-year-old widow: "One must not ignore the sensuous pleasure of ignoring an alarm and turning over once more if so inclined."

COMMENTS: "MY TIME IS MY OWN"

Time to do everything you wanted to do.

—94-year-old single woman

My problem is that I never seem to do all the things I had planned, so there is no time for boredom. However, since my time is my own, no one will complain if I complete a task on Thursday that I had planned to finish on Tuesday.

—68-year-old married man

Main attraction is not having to meet a daily set schedule. Second attraction is being able to perform activities in accordance with your physical feelings, at no required pace. Run if you feel like it. Walk if you feel like it. Sit and visit if you feel like it.

—75-year-old married man

The main attraction I find is being independent and able to do what I want when I want and not have to live by the clock. I worked for a salary for 50 years and now that I am doing volunteer work I like the freedom of choice I have as to days and hours of work. I hope to continue for a long time, for I am really a "workaholic."

—80-year-old single woman

Free as a bird.

—77-year-old single man

The chief advantage for me has been more freedom in the use of my time— an increasingly precious gift as one grows older.

—75-year-old married woman

Delightful not to have set routine. One awakens in the morning knowing one can stay in bed as long as one wishes. No need to ride in subway rush hours, plenty of time for visits to museums, theatres, and friends, to read, to walk, to spend one's time as one wishes in a relaxed fashion.

—71-year-old single woman

I can work according to my biological time clock instead of that of the business or work-a-day world.

—70-year-old widow

The new freedom of my personal schedule is a delight. I can read, take a walk, sit in the garden, take a trip, as I wish. With fewer obligations, I have gained personal tranquility which I value. I have time to enjoy my friends.

—68-year-old single man

I can allocate my time more conveniently. If I awaken around 3 or 4 a.m. rested and alert, I can use this very quiet uninterrupted time for study, practice, or composition. (I practice on my electronic organ with earphones so I don't annoy my neighbors.) A background of absolute silence is so welcome for such activity. Then I can indulge in a nap in mid-afternoon if so inclined. Couldn't do that when I had to catch a bus at 6:45 a.m. for a few a.m. lessons (private) at school.

—71-year-old divorced woman

Every day like Saturday and Sunday.

—69-year-old married man

The main attraction of retirement is that there is more time to do things, aside from work, that I want to do! I can now explore the back roads for which there was limited time before; attend weekend events without wondering when I'll do the cleaning or laundry; go look at autumn colors at their peak on a Monday; redecorate my house with plenty of time to look for items needed; visit friends and relatives living at a distance; give time for various projects or organizations as I wish; attend social or recreational events at any time without conflicts of sleep, chores, or working hours; go swimming in the middle of the morning or take a before-breakfast walk; catch appointments without regard to working hours; travel just for fun; do more reading; etc.; etc.; etc.!

—63-year-old single woman

No time clock syndrome . . .

—70-year-old married man

I do not have to be under pressure unless I overschedule myself.

—67-year-old single woman

I commuted three hours back and forth a day, and don't *miss* that *one bit!*

—68-year-old married woman

The freedom to leisurely do tasks when the "mood" develops.

—63-year-old married man

The main attraction is *time* that can be organized at will. This is an unending delight after 40 years of double-time work— namely, working while attending 11 years of college and university and then practicing a demanding profession while raising a family and meeting the needs of a busy husband and elderly parents.

—61-year-old married woman

ESSAY: AN AUTOGRAPH SESSION AT 82

Considering my age (84) and the age at which I retired (80), I would say that the main attraction of retirement is time.

Time to read a lot, which I enjoy thoroughly. Time to write a little. I have had a book of poems published, written before I retired but collected and published after retirement. Nothing could be more satisfying than an autograph session at 82 years of age.

Time to visit with friends and family and enjoy my many grandchildren and great-grandchildren. Time to revive interest in what is going on in the world through watching events and sports on television, and writing letters to columnists and broadcasters giving my viewpoint on a disputed issue or commending them when they agree with my thoughts. Time — especially this summer — to keep up with the Atlanta Braves as they were winning the Western Division pennant in the National League.

Time to do a lot of needlework, including afghans for all the new babies in the family, and an altar cloth for the church, and so on. As to the main drawback of retirement, that also is — time. Too much time when there is nothing to do. Time to think of all your aches and pains. Time to get thoroughly bored so that you worry too much, eat too much and, possibly, try to interfere too much in the affairs of family members and friends.

If I had been a different sort of person, I should have planned retirement at an earlier age, saved more towards it, and utilized that commodity, time, to much better advantage.

Some one should write a dissertation on time.

—84-year-old widow

ESSAY: "WE ARE NOW CREATURES OF WHIM"

Freedom in retirement, to be meaningful, must be followed by a preposition "from" or "to."

Taking the "from": for years I have worked for a boarding school. I chose that life deliberately, and I don't regret the decision. However, it has been an intense life, a demanding one of classes, preparations, long hours of reading and grading papers, counseling kids, coaching them in the afternoons, supervising study halls, and once a week being Officer-of-the-Day, which means checking students in at breakfast, taking care of any emergencies, and checking the dormitories to see that they are all accounted for. The job became increasingly demanding as I grew older and I was rewarded for my age by being made chairman of the discipline committee. During the '70s this committee met so frequently that I found little time for my classes (always my primary reason for teaching) and, what is worse, for my own family. No one who has not lived this life can understand its complexity and the drain on one's emotional and psychological sensibilities. I did not want to become what is popularly known as a burnt out case, and I had no aspirations to the role of a Mr. Chips. That life is over now.

Freedom "to": do simple things, go to bed when I like, arise at 5 a.m. to read, write letters, or just watch the dawn come up over our lake, enjoy friends, see my grandchildren, or go birdwatching with my wife of 41 years, or play golf. Well-meaning people ask me now that I am retired, if I'm keeping busy. The answer is, to me, obvious.

We are now creatures of whim. We can take a trip when the mood strikes us without great advance preparation — for example, a three week visit to England to see my wife's sister and family. We have always travelled that way, taking what comes on the road, and we intend to continue.

—67-year-old married man

An Overdose Of Freedom?

The previous section describes our retirees' enthusiasm for the loosening of job-related time constraints in retirement. But there's also a flip side to this freedom. Without a structure to replace the one that's dictated by full-time employment— something that most of us take for granted — retirement can be an uncomfortable experience.

A 72-year-old woman, for example, describes how, "I feel guilty at this time because I am not productive. I'm sort of like Ferdinand, just eating the daisies." And a 73-year-old widower says: "One must impose upon himself some sort of schedule in the absence of one imposed by a job. I had to learn from experience that the retiree doesn't *have* to do anything in particular and can do what he wants. I was aware of the pitfalls of this blessing, but I think it has to be lived through in order to be more than the sound of words. I was subject to a brief and mild period of despair at this point and I can imagine how paralyzing it can be for one who is hit hard. When you retire things are not the same. You have to adjust yourself to it. Keep yourself active. Do not become a wallflower. Otherwise you will slip and go downhill." In a similar vein, a 66-year-old man warns, "The main attraction of retirement is the opportunity to do what you want to do. For some, this is bliss; for others, it can be a slippery road to oblivion."

A related phenomenon is that many retirees seem to find time slipping through their fingers. According to a 72-year-old man: "While retirement does give you more time, your time tends not to be as well organized as when working. The result is you fritter your time away and you find yourself much less productive, which is a blow." A 67-year-old widower says: "Although I now have lots of time, the days can slide by so fast. I feel so much better when I can shake off any lethargy and get going on something— a project or a visit to friends or places I have always been curious about."

Of course, as retirees observe, aging and declining energy levels can be a significant reason why things don't get done as efficiently as in years past. Nevertheless, their statements suggest the strong need in retirement for "time management" skills — the ability to plan the use of one's time productively. As a 70-year-old woman observes: "It would be helpful if I had learned how to be better organized— to better manage my use of time. Could have used that skill earlier, too, but the need is more apparent when there's more time available." Some retirees make the point that "time management" may be a modern name for an age-old problem. A 70-year-old man, for example, quotes from Benjamin Franklin's *Poor Richard's Almanac:* "Dost thou love life? Then do not squander time, for that is the stuff life is made of." And another retiree mentions the Scottish proverb: "What may be done at any time will be done at no time."

Some, particularly early retirees, express the desire for time-structure by yearning for the hustle and bustle of their former jobs. Says a 63-year-old man, "I am surprised to find that I miss the challenge of not being under fairly constant pressure and of not having deadlines to meet, as was the case over the previous 35 years." A 62-year-old woman says, "Since no outside pressure on achievement is present, much self-discipline is necessary to reach the goal one sets for oneself." A 64-year-old man adds, "I miss co-workers and the hassle of problem solving. I miss working under pressure. I do my best thinking under pressure," while a 66-year-old widow admits that "theoretically, I should be self-starting. Actually, I work better when I have a deadline. The less you do, the less you do. So I am not so busy as I should be."

The need for time management skills also shows up another way— some retirees pack too many activities into the time that's available. A 73-year-woman laments, for example, having "too many irons in the fire." And a younger woman writes: "We think we have more time to use as we wish, but I find myself taking on more activities and one can really get bogged down more than when one was on a regularly scheduled work program." Overloaded schedules may simply reflect retirement jitters, according to a 69-year-old woman. "I was so apprehensive about retirement," she writes, "that I accepted offices in too many organizations. Remember that after we have worked a lifetime, we have difficulty adjusting to an extended vacation."

COMMENTS: A NEED FOR SELF-DISCIPLINE

The main thing I would have done differently to make retirement more rewarding would have been to set up some goals and priorities for activity, reading, etc. There are so many things a retiree can do that one tends to get spread a little thin.

— 78-year-old married man

Procrastination is such an evil, especially in older people. The best advice one can give to retirees is to act immediately on wishes or desires, for to put them off is to kill them.

— 73-year-old married man

I suppose that retirement's chief attraction to me is the fact that I am not governed by a strict time schedule. On the other hand, I feel that it is certainly more stimulating to have *something* to plan toward for at least one or two days each week, be it part-time employment or volunteer projects. This would present a challenge of sorts, and at the same time bring more outside interests into home life.

— 73-year-old married woman

I have friends who feel very lost without their jobs. Or others who relapse into just staying in the house reading mystery stories. Neither seems productive or content.

— 72-year-old single woman

There are still times when work piles up. That is probably my fault due to my inability to plan properly and adjust to a new situation. I found myself spending too much time on the one course I'm still teaching.

— 67-year-old widower

You begin to realize that we do not have 24 hours a day — only about five or six at the most to actually do creative, productive thinking.

— 70-year-old married man

Drawbacks: Less *incentive* for work. Less energy *because* of lack of incentive.

— 78-year-old married woman

Aside from my driving desire to complete tracing our genealogy, I know that I've been coasting, not really forcing myself to my maximum capacity.

— 75-year-old married woman

Whole new aspect of decision making. No urgency to accomplish things. Guilt feeling about idleness.

— 67-year-old widower

There is a strong tendency to relax into lethargy. Or bridge. There is a strong tendency toward compulsive volunteerism and "busywork" rather than constructive service or activity.

—*75-year-old married woman*

For an unorganized person, freedom from a schedule may be a temptation to spend too much time "relaxing."

—*70-year-old single woman*

Without the deadlines of a long working life, I find it all too easy to say mañana to everything.

—*76-year-old single woman*

"I Am My Own Boss"

Although many of our retirees indicate they enjoyed the challenges and stimulation of their jobs and miss these aspects of their work, there are aspects of their jobs they don't miss — ranging from petty annoyances to unhealthful pressures — and they make the point in many different ways. A 64-year-old woman, for example, marvels that "you don't have to wake up and face the pressures of another day at work." A 66-year-old woman tells how she's happy to be away from the "fire station atmosphere" while a 75-year-old man emphasizes relief from the "aggravations stemming from the so-called sheltered academic life."

According to a retired math professor: "There is a lifting of stress and tension from academic life, such as meeting deadlines, faculty committee service requiring research, study and writing of reports, hassling over new appointments, awarding of tenure and promotions, preparation and grading of examinations." A 72-year-old woman feels relief from "the sorts of responsibility for others that were at times awesome." Claims another woman, "My health has improved because of less tension."

Relationships with supervisors and department heads also end with retirement, and some retirees are particularly happy that they do. Says a 67-year-old man, "The best thing about retirement is that I have my freedom and can spend my time doing what *I* want to do instead of having to cater to the often uninformed ideas of superiors who had no idea what went on inside my head." A 68-year-old woman describes how she is grateful she no longer has "to answer to other people, especially when you are right and they are wrong." Says a 66-year-old widower simply: "I am my own boss."

Relationships with peers are also no longer as tense, say some retirees. In the words of a 68-year-old man: "You are no longer driven by the keen competition of business or profession. Retirees can relax and enjoy each others' company as individuals — not as power symbols. They have made their mark. They no longer have to keep proving themselves." And a 74-year-old former educator notes the "opportunity to write at one's leisure and at his own pace, and without the necessity of impressing colleagues and peers and administrators. That opportunity is one of the great benefits of retirement."

COMMENTS: "BREATHING SPACE"

Retirement gave me psychological and spiritual "breathing space," separated from the hurly-burly of the university. Ours was a particularly pressurized university atmosphere.

—67-year-old married man

No need to write reports slanted in such a way as to bring in more money for further research.

—73-year-old single man

Freedom of choice on what work I do and when. In more specific terms, freedom from the 7:45 a.m. to 5:15 p.m. work days, and 60 + hours of work I was putting in each week. Now, I work only about 30 hours a week.

—60-year-old married man

The flexibility of one's time and the freedom from 8:00 to 5:00 office schedule, including related overtime responsibilities, has for me been the most rewarding factor of retirement. Moving away from a college campus and the involvement in the related activities to a more private and relaxed lifestyle, one misses being a part of an organization and the personal relationships. But one is also released from the tensions, pressures, and deadlines.

—66-year-old married woman

No exams to make up and no papers to grade! No final evaluations of students' grades. No long boring meetings.

—66-year-old single woman

Leisure and lack of pressure. I had combined teaching and administration.

—68-year-old single woman

I have enjoyed being freed from the pressure of the annual fund raising from private sources and foundations that was necessary to run the department in the manner I felt was required. I had reached the age where long hours in the operating room tired me very much and was relieved to discontinue surgery. After many years of being "on duty" constantly it has been very pleasant to be able to plan my days to include time out for golf, travel, and cultural involvement, without feeling I was stealing the time from my job.

—80-year-old married man

Main attraction is the fact that I am master of my own time and activities. I can decide whether I want to take on a project and at what terms. I can now travel and engage in other time consuming activities when I want and how long I want. No more "rat race." I am relaxed and easy going for the first time in my life.

—78-year-old divorced man

Freedom from job insecurity and budget cuts.

—69-year-old married man

Freedom from nonsensical paper work.

—69-year-old single woman

. . . not having to solve the same business problems I was solving for 20 years.

—65-year-old divorced man

Freedom from the inexorably increasing red tape which plagues universities.

—65-year-old married man

Freedom from job-related problems and responsibilities and the "8-to-5" curse. Independence from the system (other than IRS).

—69-year-old married man

After two years I am beginning not to race my motor and gladly postpone something that might be done today until tomorrow or even next week. So far I have not felt lost or at loose ends. As someone said, I sometimes wonder how I ever found time to work. Perhaps university people never really retire — they just don't have to go to committee meetings anymore.

—67-year-old married man

Chapter 6 — ACTIVITIES

One of retirement's main attractions is leisure — a word that *doesn't* mean, as is sometimes assumed, absence of activities but *does* mean freedom to determine one's activities. As the many examples in this chapter (and throughout the book) show, people in retirement get involved in a wide variety of areas, from the arts and agriculture to Zen and zoology. Retirees also choose to work — sometimes on a volunteer basis, sometimes at a paid job — and these activities are discussed in the next chapter.

A common observation of our retirees is that the time retirement brings with it is time to do things they couldn't do before. A 70-year-old widow describes her enchantment with retirement's possibilities: "If I want to sit up half the night or more to finish a book, I can do so without having to get up early the next morning. If I want to play bridge in the afternoon, I can do so. Just the absolute freedom to do as you please, when you please, is wonderful. I thoroughly enjoyed my job at the university, and this has come after having been a partner with my husband in a business of our own, which was rather confining. Running two businesses after his death, I had not had this much time to do just what I liked to do. I can sew, draw a little (very much dabbling only), read, visit. It must be rather sinful to be able to indulge one's self this much. For instance, I am now visiting my sister and her husband halfway across the country and I've already extended my visiting time. I imagine this life would not seem so wonderful if I had not had the discipline of the working world for the past 30 years." A 64-year-old married woman notes, "My electric typewriter, new sewing machine, and bike bought *before* retirement are now being enjoyed." And a 70-year-old widower comments in his questionnaire about "hobbies galore. Would have to live 500 more years to complete my proposed projects."

Many of our retirees, such as a 64-year-old man who writes how pleased he is to have more time for "my Model-T Ford hobby," say they have cultivated interests throughout their lives which they have carried over into retirement. Some, such as a 66-year-old who describes how he recently learned to fly a glider — "something I've wanted to do since my youth"— use retirement to engage in new and sometimes long-postponed activities. As another 66-year-old observes, skills developed over long periods of time aren't always a prerequisite. He writes: "My prime interest happens to be woodworking, but long familiarity with an activity is not necessary. I have two friends who took up painting after retiring, and became ardent enthusiasts. Nor does the nature of one's interest matter. It can be anything, so long as it is absorbing." Says a 71-year-old man: "I became a potter several years before retirement and had a studio in my home. I now have a well-equipped studio in my retirement home and find it a great pleasure to turn out handsome and useful pieces which should outlast me by a thousand years. After all, pottery is non-biodegradable." Adds a 70-year-old woman: "Previous, and new, hobbies or interests can be pursued in greater depth with more time. I've had a portable loom for many years but now have more time to use it. I have even enjoyed doing more in the kitchen. Change is good in one's life, an advantage of retirement."

As illustrated in the chart, reading heads the list of retirement recreational activities. (Our survey didn't ask about television viewing or radio listening.) "Reading is a constantly renewed pleasure," is a much-repeated thought. According to an 81-year-old widower, "Books are a constant satisfaction, as is a quiet life among good neighbors." Says another man, "The first thing I did when I retired at age 65 was to join the American Association for the Advancement of Science and read *Science* cover to cover for several years. What a new education!" A 63-year-old woman writes, "I find I can do leisure reading without feeling guilty that I should be doing something else." A 78-year-old man makes this point: "It has been a pleasure to have time to read fiction and other literature in addition to professional material."

On the other side of the desk, a number of the retired were

busy writing books in their areas of expertise; a few say they are preparing memoirs and autobiographies. Retirement presents an opportunity for a 66-year-old anesthesiologist, who says, "I am now able to write a book concerned with my specialty, which I could not do in many years prior to retirement." Writing plans, however, don't always work out, according to this 78-year-old man. "I have long planned and worked toward a book on political theory, and have found that less easy to straighten out than I once expected," he comments.

THE RECREATIONAL ACTIVITIES OUR RETIREES PURSUE

(PERCENT ENGAGING IN ACTIVITY)

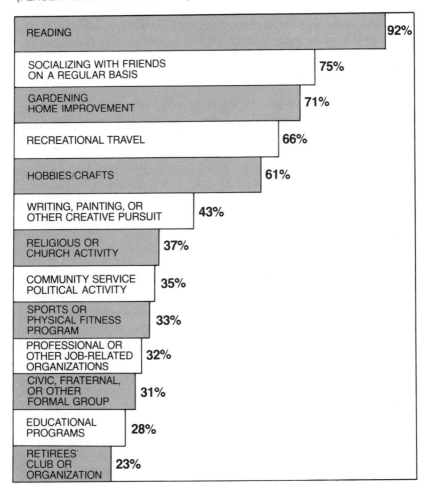

Activity	Percent
READING	92%
SOCIALIZING WITH FRIENDS ON A REGULAR BASIS	75%
GARDENING HOME IMPROVEMENT	71%
RECREATIONAL TRAVEL	66%
HOBBIES/CRAFTS	61%
WRITING, PAINTING, OR OTHER CREATIVE PURSUIT	43%
RELIGIOUS OR CHURCH ACTIVITY	37%
COMMUNITY SERVICE POLITICAL ACTIVITY	35%
SPORTS OR PHYSICAL FITNESS PROGRAM	33%
PROFESSIONAL OR OTHER JOB-RELATED ORGANIZATIONS	32%
CIVIC, FRATERNAL, OR OTHER FORMAL GROUP	31%
EDUCATIONAL PROGRAMS	28%
RETIREES' CLUB OR ORGANIZATION	23%

A number of our retirees express a special enthusiasm for travel. A 74-year-old man's comments provide an example: "I enjoy not having to be anywhere at any absolute time. For example, I could never spend time before retirement vacationing in Vermont in the fall and soaking up the beauty of the leaves. Now I can. Just returned from a three week ramble down the coast through the Carolinas, Georgia, and Florida— back through the Blue Ridge Parkway. Freedom is luxurious!" According to a 70-year-old woman, "It is such a pleasure to do what you want to do when you want to do it. I love to travel and this is one thing I had never been able to do before retirement." A 69-year-old man welcomes the "opportunity to travel without thinking of the pile-up of work at home base." And a 70-year-old woman notes one benefit that the peripatetic retiree has. "Isn't it nice," she asks, "to be able to take advantage of senior citizens' rates both at home and abroad?"

Socializing is another activity frequently mentioned by our retirees, sometimes in connection with travel. "Every day is a holiday and you can travel and see all the wonders of the world at your leisure," says a 68-year-old man. "My own area of enjoyment is golf and it's a prime source of enjoyment. In the evening, bridge and other card games are enjoyed at friends' homes. Travel and sightseeing with groups of friends make every trip a trip to be remembered." Adds a 74-year-old woman: "Mainly, I now have the time to do volunteer work, socialize, enjoy my family — especially my grandchildren. Having my husband at my side makes life very enjoyable. All is attractive to me because I keep busy, curious, and interested in life."

A large majority of our retirees portray the home as the center of retirement activities. Gardening and home improvement are often mentioned, understandably so since retirees are around their homes more than during the working years. Indeed, some say they wish they had picked up handyman skills over the years.

A 64-year-old man, for example, notes that "the outstanding attractions of retirement are, growing a garden, working on old houses, painting, and writing." Working around the house and engaging in other home-based activities remain an attraction for the following 72-year-old man, who writes: "The main attraction of retirement is being able to follow and pursue my hobbies and interests. Keeping my home repaired and attractive — I'm a do-it-yourselfer. I also have a small river place in which I spend time doing the things I think should be done — gardening, mowing, trimming, etc. Just keeping busy, but never hurrying or getting uptight. Hobbies include sound — I have cassette, reel-to-reel, and portable units and am able to spend a lot of enjoyable time in this interest. I have a second hobby — coin collecting— although this seems to be diminishing since retirement. I was not ready to retire but reached 65 at the wrong time. However, I never look back. I can really say that I have not been *bored* at any time since retirement, and I don't plan to be in the future." A 74-year-old man notes that he has "more time for reading and tinkering with mechanical things." A 71-year-old widow, however, perhaps overdid her home activities. "I had a new house built out in the country," she writes. "I worked too hard on a beautiful lawn and got a hernia."

For a 76-year-old woman, her home-based activities include "reading, watching selected programs on PBS, and listening to my recordings of classical piano and piano concertos." A 79-year-old woman describes retirement's main attractions as "having more time at home and for gardening and sewing clothes for grandchildren (particularly hand work), being free to go places with my husband, and to rest when I'm tired." And a 75-year-old man writes that he has "more time with spouse, for painting, walking with our dogs, and taking advantage of the rural location of home."

The home is often a place where retirees indulge in a variety of artistic pursuits. "I am very busy, but feel little if any pressure to produce!" says a 68-year-old woman. "I have developed new skills and have found myself creating artistic rather than 'crafty' jewelry." Says a 77-year-old man: "I started hobbies: woodworking, lapidary art, jewelry crafts. When I was 65 I purchased an electronic organ and can play classical music decently. We are opera buffs (have been members of our city's opera 20 years). I still make and give away jewelry. My wife makes afghans for her friends." A 65-year-old man tells how "Always a Sunday painter, I now have time for a concentrated effort in art activities." A 63-year-old man is particularly enthusiastic. He writes: "Presently, I'm *extremely* happy to be able to look forward to days, weeks, yes, an eternity of creative activity. I love the opportunity to draw, paint, carve, write, and design."

Even people who worked full-time at an artistic pursuit welcome the added time in retirement. Two musicians make that point. "I enjoy the leisure time to play and practice as I couldn't when I had a full-time job," says one of them, a 69-year-old woman. Says the other, a 67-year-old man, "As a composer and musician, I have much time for composing of music and the like." As the preceding quotations suggest, our retirees' artistry encompasses traditional endeavors such as painting, music, and writing. But our retirees are involved also in not-so-traditional artistic fields, such as the 60-year-old man who writes, "I enjoy developing electronic and computer circuits."

Many retirees engage in sports or physical fitness activities, although most aren't as daring as the new glider pilot mentioned at the beginning of this chapter. A 72-year-old man combined a new sport with other new activities. He tells us: "When I retired I resolved to make a break from my professional life and to seek new outlets of interest and activity. I realized that I needed to keep physically active so I learned to swim. I try to swim at least a quarter of a mile five days a week."

ESSAY: A FULL CIRCLE

During my college years I acquired interests in ancient and medieval history, philosophy, and theoretical science. Upon graduation I was not able to find a teaching spot so I returned to college and obtained a salable competence in accounting. I secured my CPA and spent nearly 15 years in public practice. Then I accepted a position at a college to teach accounting and mathematical economics.

In my academic career I was fortunate to teach a course in advanced accounting theory, which I taught from a philosophical point of view as a search for truth. This gave me all the excuse I needed to support my real interest. I am sure that my students will always remember that I wrote quotations from Aristotle and St. Thomas on the blackboard in Greek and Latin with my own translations.

This life was intellectually challenging enough to give me a great deal of satisfaction. However, I never lost interest in my three undergraduate areas of concentration, and every leisure hour I could scrape from my professional work was devoted to them. I looked forward to extended leisure to devote to them. Now I have that leisure and I am determined to pursue these interests. I think that and a loving wife is happiness.

—71-year-old married man

Many retirees mention that retirement gives them a chance to savor the outdoors, such as a 76-year-old woman who writes about "more leisure time to enjoy nature walks and field trips, as my husband and I enjoy bird watching." Or the 74-year-old widow who is happy to have the "time to enjoy the outdoors and my sheepdog." Some retirees have taken on extensive outdoor projects. "My main occupation has been outdoor work on our summer place on a lake in New England," says a 78-year-old man. "Sort-of gardening by combination of planting and selection of the native wild growths." Says an 81-year-old man: "For two or three years I missed my students and colleagues, and also the opportunity to keep abreast of developments in my specialty (a rapidly advancing field of science). However, I soon became involved in a fascinating new endeavor— that of improving the 100-year-old family woodlands. This has been a rewarding experience. If I had it to do over again, I would have gambled on a long, healthy life and had, at the start of retirement, spent more money on necessary woodworking equipment (e.g., suitable tractor) and a year at the state school of forestry!"

Retirement can also be a time to venture into new intellectual areas. "I have time to pursue hobbies, to travel, and to be
involved in an informal education program for my own enjoyment and enlightenment and not for any college degrees," says
a 62-year-old woman. Adds a man 10 years her senior: "I can
take additional educational courses that I want rather than required
courses that did not always interest me," while a 71-year-old
woman writes about "time to enjoy cooking classes and real
estate courses," and a 67-year-old widow describes the "china
painting" course she's taking. "Next month," says another 67-
year-old, "I am starting a course on computers. I have taken a
course on landscape architecture. I am presently attending a
duplicate bridge class, and serve on the travel committee of a
senior citizens group."

For the following 70-year-old woman, a continuing education program was a particularly effective way to overcome some
of her retirement problems. She writes: "I had assumed that the
main attractions of retirement would be the freedom from a set
schedule of work. In actuality, I have missed the challenge of
the extremely busy days, the no-two-days-alike aspect of the
position, and the stimulation of contacts with *people* — students,
faculty, athletes, coaches, business administrators, athletic directors. Housecleaning is a poor substitute for these personalities.
To combat the ennui, I played golf as much as I wanted to the
first summer, but when cold weather arrived something had to
be done. So I went back to school — to a university program
open to all people 65 years of age and over. Regardless of the
amount of your education, if you have a warm body and provide
three letters of character recommendation, you can attend.
The program pays the tuition and the students pay for the
books. This pursuit of further education is the most rewarding thing anyone can do during retirement. No one is too old
to learn."

Intellectual curiosity for some retirees has been channeled
into family histories. "I've particularly enjoyed tracing our own
genealogy," says a 75-year-old woman. "Starting late in life I
missed the assistance of people who could have provided me
much of the information I've had to find through research and
county and state records, etc. After eight years of community

activity, I'm withdrawing so that hopefully I can assemble my genealogical findings and share them with those others still surviving."

For some, activities in retirement are a way to cope with potentially empty days. A 65-year-old woman makes the point that, "There is no question that retirees should have active programs before retirement, to go into after retirement. A retiree doesn't find a hobby usually after retirement. It is an ennui situation. One may retire because of *being tired,* but you become more tired without a purposeful existence." According to a 63-year-old former college administrator: "Over the years I have invested in rental real estate. This now keeps me busy. The same investments in stocks or bonds would not produce activity for me." He continues: "In retirement, you must have things which need to be done — not just busy work. There are always things to be done in my real estate investments." A recurring symbol of inactivity in retirement was the rocking chair. "The tragedy of retirement is when one retires to a rocking chair," says a 71-year-old woman. In a similar vein an 81-year-old man observes: "Am now enjoying doing things I never had time to do until I retired, but the days are too short. I don't have time to use that rocking chair, which I think is good." Adds a 65-year-old man, "I believe one has to be busy, to the limits of one's ability. I think this is the secret of a happy life and retirement."

While retirees obviously enjoy such activities as hobbies, traveling, sports, and study, many happily point out that their newfound freedom also includes the opportunity to slow down or, when they want to take advantage of it, to simply do nothing. According to a 63-year-old woman, "The main attractions: Living in a rural area. Returning to the family home where I spent every vacation. Independence — being able to do things on a moment's notice and being able to change plans without jeopardizing anyone. The peace and quiet of no deadlines, no book work, no nonsense reports, no repetition of jobs. More time for hobbies both constructive and entertaining, and a chance to slow down and enjoy what God has given us." And according to a 66-year-old man, there is the "time to do the things not done during the working years: reading, traveling, hobbies, socializing — and hibernating."

Others also write that they welcome the opportunity simply to think and contemplate. For example, a 61-year-old woman comments that "retirement has afforded the time for solitude and contemplation, which was something to be desired when working." A 72-year-old woman writes about the "time to read, think, pray, write, canoe, or just do nothing." And a 90-year-old woman describes the "opportunities for much reading and listening to good music; for mild recreational exercise in lovely surroundings; for much quiet reflection and remembrance; for solitude and prayer."

COMMENTS: AN INFINITY OF ACTIVITIES

I am busy.

—70-year-old married man

I enjoy working with younger people and am an ardent sports fan, enjoying their development through the teen years and into college. Hobbies have been baseball (coaching young teams) and tennis, which I actively played until recently, when a detached retina operation affected the sight of one eye. Actively coached Pony League baseball teams until last year. Do belong to an active Retired Men's Club, which provides excellent programs and fellowship. Am on the town's recreational committee, which provides activities and sports of all kinds during the summer season and to some extent during the winter. I actively participate in community service, which has always been a major interest. Scarcely an evening goes by that I do not attend a meeting of some sort having to do with activities of all kinds.

—72-year-old single man

I live in a senior citizen apartment building and find it much fun helping to plan the various activities. I highly recommend your local senior citizens center. The one I belong to has many enjoyable day trips as well as longer trips. Join in these activities and you will find there is no boredom in retirement as long as your health is good. I keep myself busy, but when I have free time I do some sewing and enjoy arts and crafts. I find no reason for one not to enjoy retirement if they put forth a bit of effort.

—70-year-old widow

A few years before retirement a helpful suggestion came from a friend in another institution who happened to be much nearer to his retirement. What it amounted to was getting a "shoe box," cutting a slot in its cover, and putting it under one's desk as a repository for notes on things to do or topics for reading which turn up so often when there is "no time" for following up on them.

Actually, I have been reasonably busy during my retirement, since the main attraction of retirement is that one acquires a sense of freedom from a strict time schedule and scheduled obligations to others. Of course, there are limits on such a sense of freedom, limits associated with having fully adequate funds and the energy to pursue a series of possible goals. But I haven't had to resort to my shoebox.

— 79-year-old married man

Less tension, more time with family, more time with friends, more time for play, more time to read, more time for church, more time to travel where I want to go.

— 77-year-old married man

I took courses in writing and photography and now write articles and sometimes a newspaper column. Golf and swimming keep us physically fit. Travel and reading broadens our thinking. Volunteer work is its own reward.

— 73-year-old married man

Fishing and friends are a great therapy.

— 70-year-old married man

I believe one should retire while still in good health and with outside interests. Mine was, and still is, water sports.

— 69-year-old married man

Another attraction is the time to saw, chop, and rack firewood— all by hand. We save on fuel (oil) by burning wood as a supplement. The wood is free, mostly from our little grove, and I enjoy the exercise.

— 68-year-old married man

I spent no money on alcohol or tobacco. I spent it on a 22-foot sailboat. I enjoyed it for several years before retirement and take it out two or three times a year now. If the things I enjoy more now become unavailable to me, I would use the boat more. It has a galley, head, and berths for five and it can be in the water on a lake 10 miles from home in an hour or so. The comradeship of other boaters is there for me if I need it. I keep up my membership in the U.S. Power Squadron, attend most of the meetings, and teach boating to members and the public.

— 74-year-old married man

I was lucky enough to come to know both France and Italy well during my working years, and now if I feel bored or stale, I just take a trip there. I have just finished a stay in Italy, dipping once again into their art, their music, their literature, their language.

— 68-year-old unmarried man

I am a great believer in physical activity after retirement. I think that it is very important to have something that involves work with your hands. I have built two houses— a guest house and the house in which we live. I am now involved in landscaping the yard and tending the garden. Aside from keeping busy with work outside, since retirement I have found time to do the reading that I never had time to do before. I have also found time to do some thinking. It is satisfying to have found a way of thinking about the philosophical and psychological problems of life, and to be able to discuss such thoughts with others.

—78-year-old married man

The main attractions for me are having the freedom to do what I want to do each day— being able to enjoy my wife's company, and not having to meet a time schedule, and being able to afford the luxury of meeting friends for breakfast, brunch, or dinner. As for the drawbacks, I have none. I am so busy with mowing the lawn, gardening, and maintenance work around the home that I am not bored, and when not working around our home, I hunt, fish, play golf, play bridge, etc.

—71-year-old married man

More time to square dance.

—69-year-old married man

My many interests and activities resulted in growing friendships in many fields and participating in various programs, from archaeological excavations and concerts (not rock!) to aiding in church-sponsored chicken barbeques!

—68-year-old married woman

In my case, it helps that I still have my main lifelong activity as a part of me: my art and state of being as a scholar. Teaching was fulfilling and rewarding, but was only an application of my lifelong personal development.

—60-year-old married man

In golf, we have set goals of improvement. This has been stimulating and rewarding. There is also much socialization in golf.

—73-year-old married man

I've discovered that I am basically lazy, therefore I like not having to do anything unless I truly like to do it. I love to read, sew, and play bridge. Opportunities abound, either alone for the first two or with my friends, also retired, for bridge and companionship.

—69-year-old widow

Freedom and ability to travel— 49 states, 42 countries.

—73-year-old married man

Travel = Japan, Russia, Europe, South Pacific (New Zealand, Australia, Tahiti, Fiji).

—78-year-old married woman

During the last eight to 10 years of working I seemed always to be looking forward to vacations and weekends and then found them too short. We now live in Southern California six months, and in New Hampshire five months and spend two weeks crossing the country late spring and late fall each year. We've also taken several trips abroad and plan more.

—66-year-old married man

Have visited every continent, including making 10 trips to Europe and three trips to Hawaii— plus Alaska— in the past 10 years.

—69-year-old single woman

Retirement gives us freedom for mobility— to England twice in five years, to China last summer, to the Midwest this month.

—73-year-old married woman

I wanted to learn something about music, so I took a course in fundamentals of music and I'm learning how to play the piano.

—72-year-old married man

I found time to return to college and after an intensive six-week course was certified as a master gardener, this after having been a horticultural grad for nearly 50 years.

—71-year-old married man

Perhaps if we had it to do over we might have traveled more when we first retired and could have more easily stood the strain of travel. If the husband or wife is a member of any group or organization they should continue their membership and take an active part in it. It is a mistake to sever such connections. We made every effort to plan for our retirement, and this, plus reasonably good health, has contributed greatly to a happy retirement.

—85-year-old married man

I am happier in retirement than I was when I was teaching. Perhaps this is because teaching was never my full life— that is, I always had my own special interests and activities. I always enjoyed reading, not just in my field of teaching, but in many areas of interest and concern. Thus, when I gave up teaching I did not give up my interests and my concerns. In fact, I was freer than before to follow my own personal bent.

—71-year-old married man

. . . having more time to devote to my deep interest in book collecting.

—69-year-old married man

I can be with my family and I can see my friends, locally and in the South, many of whom now live in Florida.

I can read. I greatly enjoy keeping up with the current scene in foreign affairs, religion, politics and the stock market. I am tremendously concerned with the resolution of conflict by non-violent means and the building of a peaceful world.

I can correspond with friends. I have a large circle of friends with whom I keep in touch. Letters contribute greatly to my happiness, including the letters from a young Asian youth whose education I have sponsored for six years. He is now 16 and attending trade school.

I can rest when I feel ill or tired.

I can savor life itself. I can pause to watch the sunset or linger idly with friends on a summer evening.

I can play games. I like to solve crossword puzzles, jig saw puzzles, almost any kind of puzzles and to participate in a friendly game of cards or scrabble.

I can make some personal contribution to the comfort, happiness or well-being of others. I am able to spend time each week driving a handicapped person to do errands, taking a woman who doesn't drive to see her hospitalized husband, calling on shut-in persons, taking foreign students who have no car to see places of scenic beauty or historical interest located in this part of the state.

I can travel with the seasons, living always where temperatures are within my comfort range, and where paths and pavements are safe for a walker in winter. These seasonal trips permit leisurely travel North with the Spring, opportunities to see places of interest along the way, and to revel in the panorama of color of a Vermont autumn.

—72-year-old widow

Looking at TV sports without a guilty conscience.

—73-year-old married man

Leisure to enjoy your leisure.

—79-year-old married man

Chapter 7: WORKING AND HELPING

Working For Pay And Pleasure

In addition to the many activities described in the previous chapter, many of our retirees choose to work in retirement. They have done so by continuing pre-retirement work activities, such as teaching, lecturing, consulting, research, writing, and other professional duties, or by applying their pre-retirement skills in new ways. In a few cases, retirees seem to have changed job interests altogether.

Just under half of our retirees say they have worked for pay after retirement. Of those who worked, about 10% returned to work only to earn extra money. About a third of those who worked say they did so solely for nonfinancial reasons — they enjoyed their jobs or wanted to keep themselves occupied, for example — and about half say they worked for a mixture of financial and nonfinancial reasons.

In some cases, our retirees continued in a modified form of their pre-retirement jobs and willingly did so without pay. Writes a 69-year-old emeritus professor in the engineering field: "I have the advantage of being granted the privilege of a shared, but virtually private, office and telephone in my former department, in exchange for which I gladly donate my services to supervise a couple of ongoing research projects and graduate students, and to pass on experience to younger faculty members. I enjoy these contacts and do not need to be reimbursed for this time. Basically, I am not really 'retired' — in my wife's eyes — because I continue to engage in professional activities. I not only provide guidance to grad students but I also engage in engineering consulting and I attend professional society meetings." According to a 71-year-old former professor who also forgoes a paycheck: "I keep in touch with my former department at the university, taking care of book orders, advising graduate students, and supervising their dissertations. This kind of activity is more challenging than teaching regular classes, particularly on the undergraduate level." And for a 74-year-old scientist, the only attraction of retirement he notes is his donated time "working at the mollusk department at my university's zoological museum."

More often, however, the retirees who continued at their former jobs or at related jobs did so for pay, although remuneration was rarely mentioned as the primary motive. Some, like the following 77-year-old, continued to work at their pre-retirement jobs, but at a slower pace and in a way that eased them into full retirement. He writes: "After I reached 65, and was retired by the school as a matter of policy, I was asked to stay on part-time for one more year. For 11 more years I was asked each year to stay on 'one more year,' which I did, teaching four full classes five days a week, but with none of the extra duties I had previously had (assistant headmaster, admissions, coaching, etc). I thoroughly enjoyed keeping my contacts at school and still getting home for a late lunch with my wife. More and more I felt that I was needed at home (my wife was ill) and we also wanted to do more traveling in the fall and spring."

Some retirees dwell on the advantages of what amounts to part-time retirement. A 74-year-old man describes how, "I spend the cold months at the university, continuing my laboratory research in biochemistry. In the growing season we go to our summer house and acreage where we work on our respective projects. My wife is converting a glen into a wild flower garden. This involves changing the course of a small stream, making pools, and then searching for and planting wild flower plants indigenous to the region. For my part I am finishing a cabin I built, am planting trees, and keeping the entire place in repair. I also care for a small orchard. My winter months at the university keep me in contact with younger investigators who are generating new ideas. I also participate in other university activities, when I wish to. I am fortunate in having the best of all worlds in retirement."

A 67-year-old secretary makes related points. She says, "I still work at my former job three days a week because I enjoy my work and my fellow employees." She adds: "However, on the

INCIDENTALLY: SOCIAL SECURITY AND THE WORKING RETIREE

Our retirees frequently gave thanks to Social Security's indexing of benefits to rates of inflation, especially when those rates are high. However, a few who are working also grumble about another provision of the Social Security program — its so-called Earnings Test that trims the Social Security benefits of any recipient under the age of 70 who earns more than a certain dollar amount per year from paid employment. This dollar amount is keyed to changes in average national wages, and is different for people aged 65 to 70 and those under 65. In 1984, it was $6,960 and $5,160, respectively, for people in those age categories. Those earning more than these limits must give up $1 in Social Security benefits for every $2 of their "excess" income from employment.

The earnings test incensed one 67-year-old man for what he calls its "absolute unfairness." Observing that he is also paying Social Security and income taxes at the same time he is losing Social Security benefits, he demands, "Where is the common sense in that law?" Likewise, a 67-year-old married woman praises Social Security as "a godsend for senior citizens." But, she adds, the Social Security laws "should not penalize seniors who want and need to work to supplement their income. The earnings level should be lifted and persons in good health should be encouraged to work as much as possible. The income is helpful and the business world contact is good mental and physical therapy." Another man of the same age, engaged in consulting work, wonders whether he should not have delayed retiring until he was 70 and could earn unlimited amounts without forfeiting any Social Security benefits.

days I don't work, I love the feeling of freedom. It's almost like playing hookey." Says a 67-year-old former college professor: "The main attractions are simply time to do more things for pure pleasure and to teach part-time without the burden of multiple preparation and the correction of freshman themes." According to a 71-year-old man, a former teacher in a private school who now works part-time as a school librarian: "To me this is a very satisfactory way of life. No financial worry. Doing useful work that I enjoy, yet without many of the pressures of full-time work. No work to take home at night. The feeling of being useful and busy are most important. The older I get, I am more and more convinced of the need for people to work as long as they possibly can."

The following 66-year-old woman, a typist at a research library, wants to continue part-time work at her institution for a particularly special reason. "Since I am severely handicapped— I'm a wheelchair bound paraplegic— I have always considered my position as therapeutic as well as financially rewarding and feel that the therapy of work is needed for my survival. My life revolved around my job and, upon retirement, I was able to secure a part-time position in the same department at the library. This has worked out satisfactorily for me so far. But if I could change things, I would prefer to keep my full-time job— tapering off a day at a time over a period of a couple or more years instead of cutting from a 40-hour to a 12-hour part-time job, such as I have now."

Among the reasons the retirees cite for continuing to work are a need to remain active in retirement, to continue pursuing lifelong interests, and, simply, to contribute to society. According to a 66-year-old psychologist: "I am not fully retired, nor ever expect to be, as long as I can maintain my clinical psychology practice. I had not planned my part-time private clinical practice as a valuable feature of my retirement years when I started it 25 years ago, but that is what it has become. So I have lucked out in having a lifelong career which can be adapted at will to my physical and other circumstances, which is socially useful, and in which my satisfaction seems to be matched by my increasing skills. Age does bring some compensatory wisdom, perhaps." A

65-year-old chemist explains how, "I have set up my chemical consulting business so that I can work as much or as little as I wish. I enjoy what I am doing because I feel I am helping our community, our state, and even our country."

In explaining her decision to work in retirement, an 84-year-old former music professor emphasizes the need to be active. She points out that while retirement's "attractions include time for reading, travel, and pursuits for which work routine left no time before," retirement's drawbacks include the possibility that "eventually there may be *too* much time to be filled. That is one reason I returned to teaching music part-time to both college and local students, taking only the number of students that would provide work without pressure or loss of leisure time. As my health began to fail, I was able to take fewer students. I did not quit teaching until a doctor ordered me to do so at age 82."

Some retirees entered new fields. That was the case with a 60-year-old former administrator of nursing services. She writes: "I became a salesman for a home products company three years after forced retirement and it has enhanced all facets of my life — spiritual, personal, and financial." Some start up a new business, like the 68-year-old man who says that, "I was afraid of doing just nothing. So I started a consulting practice in toxicology." Others wish, in retrospect, they had set up a business. A 79-year-old man, for example, comments, "In later years of paid employment, I should have developed a small business or a professional practice in order to have more regularized activity. Not for current income as such."

A few retirees entered new fields because they really didn't retire — they simply switched careers. For example, a 73-year-old former college teacher originally retired at age 55 from an industrial firm. "I wanted to do other things besides what I was doing to make money, and prove to myself I could be successful in a new career of teaching that I thought would be more rewarding. It was and still is," he recalls, adding, "I'm disappointed with some of my peers who accepted teaching as just a job. Thank God there were, and are, those who are dedicated." The comments in "Three People, Nine Careers" provide additional examples of multiple retirement due to career-switching.

ESSAYS: THREE PEOPLE, NINE CAREERS

I retired as a superintendent of public schools at 55 and went into college-level teaching and administration. I have a third career in the travel business and I still work six days a week (part-time) and I adjust my schedule as I see fit. Early retirement does penalize one in terms of the amount of benefits available compared to those who retire later. This, however, is offset by the additional income which can be earned if you are still young enough for a second career. I do not regret having played it as I did.

— 68-year-old married man

I've had a very successful career for 20 years as a TV producer and a successful and rewarding career for nine years as a professor. Retiring from teaching has permitted me to have a career as an actor in soap operas, commercials, films, etc. and my current career is both successful financially and fun. Check me in another seven years. I may be having yet another career.

— 73-year-old married man

Since retiring for the third time on January 1, 1982, I work part-time 24 hours a week. I now have more time for golf, fishing, sight-seeing, and picnics, and can spend more time with my wife of 42 years. I retired from the Navy in 1957 knowing I could get a good position in police work. I owned my home, knew I didn't have to move again unless I wanted to, and that my wife and children would remain in the same home and attend the same school. I retired from the police department in 1968 and moved to Hawaii, where we had previously lived. After several months of not working, I decided to go back to work so I could qualify for Social Security. I have been on the college staff, first full-time and now part-time, for 12 years.

— 66-year-old married man

Work activities for some retirees involve politics and government. A 71-year-old former college professor, for example, describes how "the main attraction of retirement includes a chance to get into new fields of endeavor. Two months after retirement from college, I became mayor and enjoy politics immensely." Another 71-year-old man, a horticulturist who had been in charge of a university's ground maintenance and development department, now advises a local botanical garden on a volunteer basis and also serves as a paid community representative for a state assemblyman. And a 66-year-old points to the advantages of working on a state commission, a position which he says provides both financial and nonfinancial benefits: "I have had the opportunity to do what I enjoy — teaching, research, and administration. And now in retirement I serve (by Governor's appointment) on a state-wide commission which sets natural resource management policy. It is real world involvement with issues that touch all the people."

In the main, though, our retirees' work in retirement seems to be more typically related to pre-retirement work. For example, a 60-year-old, who retired early, went back to work to help out "a department head, who is a good friend, when he requested help teaching math at a local college because of staff shortages." A 66-year-old woman, who had been active in health service, is now involved part-time with "hospital epidemiology and infection control." (Interestingly, she adds, "My spouse, who is partially retired, is designing a retirement center, and this project is rewarding to both of us.") Another woman, age 70, who had been a bookkeeper at a college, plans to work "as a bookkeeper for a needlework shop that is about to open." She also works at her former institution "at the beginning of semesters."

There are more examples. A 78-year-old former college consortium administrator works as a part-time paid fund raiser for his alma mater. An 84-year-old woman, formerly in hospital administration, serves in retirement as her hospital's historian and curator of its hospital museum. And a 73-year-old former college educator in radio management is producing, on a voluntary basis, a radio program that "we hope is serving not only senior citizens but also those who one day *will be* senior citizens."

The following *Comments* section contains other examples of people who, although retired, have continued to earn income from work, either for nonfinancial reasons or for a combination of nonfinancial and financial reasons. Most of the statements are from men who formerly held faculty or other professional jobs. This reflects survey findings that proportionately more men than women worked for pay at some time in retirement, and that professionals are more likely than other occupational groups to continue or resume working after they retired. Some people continue professional "work" in another sense— although unpaid, they continue pre-retirement activities such as research and writing just for the enjoyment and intellectual stimulation of doing so.

COMMENTS: "I WONDER IF I AM REALLY 'RETIRED'"

So far, I have had the good luck to be invited to teach, contribute scholarly articles to symposia on topics of great interest to me, and to attend as many conferences and professional meetings as I would have wished. Currently, I am giving a series of public lectures as the holder of a named writing professorship in a fine university and will teach there on a full-time basis in the first half of 1983.

I am realistic enough not to expect that I can maintain my present post-retirement level of participation in the work of the academic community in coming years. I see no sharp falling-off but only the prospect that self-discipline (or the lack of it) will determine how high that level of participation will be.

— 70-year-old former college faculty member

I do not have the routine of nine hours of teaching a week, but there are more lectures and undertakings that I have to choose between and more time to read and to write than I had in my closing years of teaching, where the academic pattern compelled endless committee meetings and the department demanded all kinds of attention. I have found that fathering three books and half a dozen pamphlets— I have lost count of the number of introductions to books and opportunities to lecture— has given me more than ample scope in my retirement.

— 81-year-old former college administrator

My former employer still uses my services on a part-time basis, at my option.

— 69-year-old former college faculty member

I taught for 30 years in a sheltered environment, in a top-grade secondary school where my peers were dedicated to teaching and to students. During those very busy years, I could only give retirement a few "scary" moments of thought in which I wondered how I'd live on the reduced income. For some reason I did not become depressed at my income situation and when the time came I went to work part-time in order to earn the extra money I needed. I found that I could cope and be interested in a job that involved little mental strain. I organized the files for a franchise company, researched clients for a big corporation, and made a chart of incomes for a union to submit to the government. Thus, I can suggest to future retirees to keep busy, even if at first you think it is a menial task. All jobs are menial at times. From my vantage point today, I realize retirement has been a wonderful experience.

— 92-year-old former private school faculty member

If a person desires, as I did, to keep their office for a while and the university has the ability to grant it, then that to me is the ultimate. The trauma of a break from campus schedule to retirement was lessened by my being able to use my office, and the advantages of the university, to finish my research. They have kindly let me keep my office for these past six years and it has been a most satisfying experience. I have completed some research and will have a book published soon.

— 71-year-old former college faculty member

Retirement enabled me and my wife to start building our institute on the causes of war and the conditions of peace.

— 71-year-old former college faculty member

The lecture circuit has been interesting in both socially and professionally developing my contacts. It also enhances my writing. I am sending my third book to publishers this month and will revise two others. I am still attending seminars and symposia, taking courses to keep my scientific training up-to-date.

— 65-year-old former chemist

I am particularly fortunate in my retirement because I still have my office and laboratory to continue my scientific research without pressure to obtain grants, meet deadlines, or publish papers.

— 74-year-old former college faculty member

I was offered a secretarial position which I could not resist because the people were so nice and their office only four blocks from my home.

— 80-year-old former secretary

I was actively engaged in writing and editing a set of Latin text books. The books require constant revising (and bring in fairly generous royalty payments annually) and now, as a widower since March, I am fortunate to have this activity continue.

— 77-year-old former college faculty member

Early in my teaching career I enjoyed teaching creative writing in the junior high school. After retirement I worked with small groups of 6th, 7th, and 8th graders on writing, and wrote myself. In these small groups we read our pieces to the group. In 1980 I put together a pamphlet of poems that I had printed and distributed to friends. This gave me great pleasure. Two years ago, I taught a free course on short stories to senior citizens. A class of about 15 met in the local library. I supplied the text for classic short stories. We read one story a week. I am doing the same thing now with a new text of modern short stories.

— 77-year-old former private school faculty member

Chief satisfaction has been the freedom to continue the life I had led with occasional frustrations for near 50 years, the life of a humanist scholar. I have been able to write two books, one deriving from my scholarly work, the other from the war experiences of my family. (This a direct product of the effort to prepare a mass of family papers for deposit in public archives.) I have also given some 500 old and rare books to a university library, and am preparing much of my personal correspondence and research collections for a similar purpose.

— 82-year-old former college faculty member

I do not believe in forced retirement at any age, as long as the person can do the work and wants to. I have already retired from two university jobs, but I intend to continue my work as a psychotherapist and marriage and family counselor as long as possible.

— 75-year-old former college administrator

I retired early because I wanted to devote my full attention to study and freelance writing. This was not primarily to make money, but because I felt that I could make a useful contribution in that way, and wanted to do so. I still feel that it was the right decision. In one sense, I am not really retired — that is, I still devote myself to my work, though I suppose I do take more time off, since if I want to take a trip, or do something at home one day, I can do so.

I still have an office at the university where I previously worked (provided by the university), although I am not on their payroll. I make use of the library there also. I have the opportunity to meet with students or do some part-time teaching if I want to do so. So far I have chosen not to teach any full class, but have filled the role of occasional visiting lecturer without pay. My primary attention is devoted to study and writing — which I did before retirement but which I can now pursue without the distractions of teaching and administration. This is why I wonder if I am really "retired." I do receive a pension, but am still working as a self-employed writer. Retirement will be gradual, in the form of reduction of hours of work.

— 66-year-old former college faculty member

I quit the faculty of a state university according to the rules, at 65, and then was immediately appointed a visiting professor in a private college and my employment there continued annually for nine years. I had recently completed a little textbook. When I retired I started on a trade book, so I experienced no break except that I had no teaching and no institutional duties. I kept myself busy in libraries and at the typewriter for some eight years, and afterward had only occasional writing assignments — articles for encyclopedias, book reviews, and the like.

—89-year-old former college faculty member

So far I have enjoyed my retirement quite well. Our university has permitted me to teach a course each term, and as I have always enjoyed young people I have elected to teach elementary physics for people who have little background in both the field and in mathematics. The time allows me also to work at some spectroscopy which I could not do while I was in the Dean's office. I enjoy students, and I think they enjoy me — so I am quite happy. Both the department and I will determine when I am no longer suitable for the job.

—72-year-old former college faculty member

As a retired college president I have been extremely fortunate in my decade of retirement. I have an office on the campus, a half-time secretary, and more than enough activities (both within the university and on the outside) to keep me comfortably busy without the burdens and responsibilities of administrative office.

—79-year-old former college administrator

A Barrier To Work

A small number of our retirees — about 10% of those who worked since retiring or 4% of all the retirees — report they have run into difficulty finding suitable work. One principal problem, at least as perceived by some, is age stereotyping — an automatic downgrading of a person's abilities and skills because of age and retired status.

For example, a 68-year-old man, who taught at both the college and secondary school level, says: "The main drawback of retirement is that because of my age I am written off. I would not be considered for a teaching position although I know more of my field now than ever. My health is still satisfactory, but I am just not considered." And a former college professor and dean who retired at 65 but continued on a consulting assignment recalls how, "When I became 70, I was dropped as a consultant — probably for age." He adds: "I am not sure that the clock is a good measure of an individual's ability to perform. I think I am a more patient and thoughtful teacher now than when I began at barely age 25, after my Ph.D."

Some retirees who commented about age biases are unhappy, not only because their skills are being neglected but because they believe society is missing a valuable opportunity. A 72-year-old woman, a former secretary, suggests that "ways need to be found to use this reservoir of talents, skills, and abilities productively and usefully and not just charitably or voluntarily." Another 72-year-old woman has the following suggestion: "I have tried hard to work as a volunteer in my field, teaching, but have been unable to find work either as a teacher or a tutor. I wish an organization would organize us teachers willing to continue teaching on a voluntary basis in the same way retired businessmen are called upon to lend a hand to small business ventures. Then there would not be this waste of good human material. Perhaps we will learn one day to appreciate and value the experience and wisdom of our older population."

A 68-year-old former college administrator — who complains that "the denigrating image that society casts on the elderly, i.e., those out of the job market forever, becomes psychologically destructive"— suggests a job-hunting strategy. She explains: "Looking back, I would have secured, if possible, a part-time position before cutting loose from full-time employment. The possibilities of securing such work are far greater than when you are already retired, because in retirement you are considered to be in the heap of has-beens, or at least are viewed in that sense, erroneous though it may be."

Some retirees feel that when they do get a job in retirement they risk being exploited. The 72-year-old former secretary mentioned above, for example, states: "I did not like being asked to work part-time at minimum pay and no benefits, yet be expected to provide output equal to a regular employee, just *because* I was retired. Many retired workers are asked to come back to do the *same* job, or even a *special* job because of ability and experiences, yet do not receive equal base pay. This is more the case with women. Men fare better by calling such work 'consulting' or some such designation." And according to a 67-year-old widow: "The institution where I taught had an age 65 mandatory retirement age. I thought, and still think, this was unfair because I was teaching effectively and they hired me back at one-third my previous salary to do one-half my previous job. Clearly my work was not in question. This did blight my retirement."

The age discrimination that some retirees perceive also affects them in another way — in feelings of alienation. Some of these views are captured in the *Comments* section below.

COMMENTS: "PLEASE DISAPPEAR"

No longer part of the mainstream of society, especially so for the professional. The public attitude on the part of the employed toward retirees is deplorable, and is one of the American social deficiencies, i.e., "Mr. Retired Person, please disappear."

—76-year-old married man

I think, too, that the current emphasis on "gerontology" puts retired people into a special category that isolates us from those who are still working. Caring for the elderly may be a form of compassion, but I wish it were not becoming such a growth industry.

—75-year-old married woman

The main disadvantages are: being left out of the world of action, being viewed as a spectator rather than as a participant, being expected to step aside to make room for younger blood, and being numbered among the "oldies" who have nothing left to contribute to society.

—66-year-old married man

The present policy is rather strange. Before retirement a professional person is much admired and sought for his contributions etc., but as soon as he retires he is forgotten as though he is a changed person.

—69-year-old married man

The drawbacks include: becoming part of that group of people who are no longer wanted in the work force, having employers and government deciding what you can and cannot do because of age and Social Security regulations, facing the stereotype of the "senior citizen." Suddenly, in one day, you have become a person who is not supposed to think for yourself and have any money, and must jump on the bandwagon of those who are looking for "give-aways" and benefits. To me this is degrading and ridiculous.

—69-year-old single woman

Attractions of retirement: To be more a *citizen of the world*. Drawbacks of retirement: Not to be *part of the nation*.

—83-year-old single woman

The retiree needs recognition— an individual recognition— as opposed to the recognition that he/she is now part of that vast horde of humanity we call seniors, senior citizens, golden-agers, snowbirds, etc. During our working days we were contributing. Now, it seems, we're more tolerated than needed.

—67-year-old married man

Voluntary Work: "A Little Rent For Your Place In The World"

The work interests of retirees are in addition to a wide variety of traditional voluntary or charitable services that they provide. Half of our retirees perform charitable or volunteer service, often expressing great satisfaction about their involvement in these activities. "Voluntary work gave me the opportunity to devote my unused talents in ways I wanted to use them, but was unable to because of the kind of work I was involved in," writes a 75-year-old married woman. Says an 80-year-old woman, "I think retirees must continue to contribute to their communities as long as possible. That volunteer work will keep you stimulated— and it will help you pay a little rent for your place in the world." And a 70-year-old man suggests that retirees "initiate a creative activity, writing in particular. Enroll in adult cultural study programs, especially a study of music appreciation and study piano playing! If any time is left— volunteer!"

Most of our retirees devote less than 10 hours a week to providing volunteer services. There are exceptions, of course. A 75-year-old woman notes that she spends 30 hours a week providing volunteer services, adding, "I average 10 hours, plus or minus, for each of three agencies" involved with charitable and health matters. This retiree has also founded a community voluntary action group.

Women were somewhat more likely than men to become involved in philanthropic work — almost 60% of the women retirees (including 70% of the single women) compared to 45% of the men. Our retirees' voluntary and charitable services cover a wide variety of activities, as the chart indicates. A single woman in her 70s, for example, writes: "My lifetime hobbies of reading, music (listening and performing), crocheting, etc. filled my leisure hours when I was active. But these are not sufficient for sociability with those who do not share my interests or have such handicaps as deafness and blindness. Therefore, I'm making an effort to broaden my activities by participating in such experiences as taking blind, deaf, or other handicapped persons for walks or other pursuits which they may enjoy."

An 85-year-old woman comments: "I became involved in the community, serving as president of both the women's club and the local historical society, working in the library, and serving church suppers. Perhaps I was easily 'amused', but I enjoy my life and my community." Adds a 74-year-old woman: "I have been helping as interpreter and friend to South American children and their families at a cancer research foundation of a children's hospital." The range of volunteer activities is further exemplified by an 81-year-old widower who says "the local library has busied me as trustee, etc., for the past decade"; a 71-year-old man who spends a portion of his week as a "volunteer in a hospice program"; and a 70-year-old widow who helps out "at a telephone center for the deaf."

Church-related activities are a focal point for many volunteer services. "I thoroughly enjoyed my work for many years. I am able to put those same talents to work in my home and church," says a 61-year-old woman. A 69-year-old woman comments, "Church activities have always had high priority in our lives, so now we are free to devote as much time as we wish to these activities. Bible study groups and children's Bible club ministry occupy much of my time." Adds a 65-year-old man, "I enjoy working with our church and with various charitable organizations. We are attempting to rehabilitate at least 11 homes for low-income families."

PHILANTHROPIC ACTIVITIES OUR RETIREES ENGAGE IN

Type of Volunteer or Charitable Service	Percentage of Retirees Involved*
Community/civic activities (e.g., United Way, Girl Scouts)	**28%**
Educational/cultural services (e.g., Headstart, museum, library volunteer)	**27%**
Help church, synagogue, other religious organization (e.g., Sunday school teacher, choir director)	**27%**
Hospital or health services	**15%**
Help older people (e.g., Meals on Wheels driver, aide at senior citizens center)	**13%**
Other (e.g., aid government and private social agencies, work at election polls, provide counseling services)	**14%**

*Percentages total over 100% because retirees say they are involved in more than one form of volunteer or charitable work.

At the same time that our retirees describe their interests in volunteer work, they express a caution about it. An 80-year woman writes: "You may be inclined to get into too many organizations because you feel the need to be doing things. Many retired people volunteer too much of their time and find that they have too little time for themselves. There is so much that needs to be done for others. Your body wants to slow down but you still feel the need to be very active."

Others complain that misperceptions about retired people may lead to a misunderstanding about their availability for volunteer service. "People seem to believe that once retired you have nothing to do and therefore are available to take part in and be available for every oddball senior activity," says a 77-year-old man. A 70-year-old woman agrees: "People think you have nothing to do and insist that you join every organization and assume too many responsibilities." Echoes a 78-year-old widow: "It is easy to become too deeply involved in too many community projects. People are inclined to want to work a willing horse to death." Adds a 65-year-old man: "I am ambivalent about the attitude of the community: 'Now that you are retired, we want you to lecture, volunteer your services, organize and run workshops, work in political campaigns — all without salary or honorariums, of course.' It is good to be appreciated and wanted but I feel that I have been giving all and receiving little."

On balance, however, many of our retirees have learned how to adjust to the demands of voluntary activities. According to a 76-year-old woman, "The 'plus' of retirement includes release of my time for useful projects. I have always tried to spend some hours doing volunteer work — now I fill my days with it and still find time to socialize with friends." Adds a 68-year-old man: "It is pleasant to be able to plan and participate in volunteer and civic activities — hospital board, blood bank, elderly planning for housing, programs for school children, president of the country club, class chairman for college, consultant to former company, church, fund drives in community, garden club, and small wage-earner activities."

ESSAY: "A SENSE OF BEING OF SERVICE"

I have always had an interest in physiography and the environment. Then as I grew older I developed an interest in the then-relatively new field of gerontology. Retirement gave me the opportunity to delve more deeply into these diverse fields.

Because I developed a modicum of expertise in environmental problems, I was invited to serve on various boards and commissions as a public member — first county, then state, national and international. These were gratifying opportunities for continued growth and association with stimulating people, and provided a sense of being of service — aspects I had feared to lose when no longer part of an active college faculty. The work required volumes of fine reading and as eyesight deteriorated prior to cataract surgery I either resigned or did not accept re-appointment. But through the League of Women Voters I can still serve on my regional interleague environmental group.

My experience as a student of gerontology preceded the explosion of public interest in the field and related government programs, so that I found myself one of only a few qualified persons in the sparsely populated part of the state in which I lived. In successive years I either taught gerontology as an extension of the university to nurses, social workers, and volunteers to whom working with older adults was new, or conducted brief training sessions throughout my portion of the state. These are now finished; there are now quite a few qualified younger people and the government programs include training.

But in one area — bereavement counseling — either on a one to one basis or in groups, there continues to be a need I can fulfill. This led to my association with a hospice to help the volunteers who care for families following the death of the patient. Once again it is a sense of being of service that is the reward.

—79-year-old widow

Chapter 8: DOLLARS AND CENTS

Financial Matters

A pivotal part of retirement preparation involves finances — planning to have sufficient funds to make the most of the retirement experience— and, indeed, our retirees' comments contain many references to income and other financial matters. Our retirees view finances and health (discussed in the next chapter) as the two most critical factors shaping the retirement experience.

The importance of an adequate level of retirement income was mentioned by retirees at all income levels*. A 74-year-old man with a relatively low income of $7,500, for example, notes: "I think the main factor of retiring is being financially able to retire. So you won't have to just sit around and not be able to do the things you were used to doing when you were working and had a regular paycheck. To be able to buy the things you need — for entertainment, travel, home needs, and health." Another man, also 74 but with a much higher income of $50,000, observes: "One of the main attractions is the *freedom* to do what I want when I want to. Which brings me to one of the main essentials of retirement and that is *money*. To enjoy retirement freedom one has to have the financial strength to do so."

Admonitions like these are a common refrain. An 83-year-old man, with an income of $10,000, writes: "We should spend less and save more for retirement. True, we don't know what the future holds for us but should not think of just today. We must plan as if we know there is a tomorrow. So that if we are

---

* The retirees were asked to report their annual income by indicating the income range in which it fell. They could choose from 12 income ranges progressing from under $5,000 to over $50,000. They were asked to report total household income, including separate income of spouses. When we mention a retiree's income in this chapter, we are referring to the upper end of the reported income range.

blessed enough to see it, we will be prepared." Says a 71-year-old man with an income of $20,000, "Save as much money as you can to be independent." According to a 68-year-old widow, who says her income is $25,000 a year, "I must now husband my income very carefully just to maintain a base living. Retirement has many attractions, I believe, but if one cannot afford them in retirement what good is retirement? Having the time to do things is little satisfaction if one cannot afford to pursue them." Adds a 77-year-old man with an income of $30,000, "Only with a fair degree of financial competence to rely upon can a retiree expect to savor the relaxing experience of retirement."

Across all income ranges also, our retirees write that they have had to make some financial adjustments to retirement. An 83-year-old married man, with a $10,000 income, observes: "The attractions and the drawbacks of retirement are what you make it. We do the things we want to by planning. Our wants are within our income. We enjoy what we can afford and do not do what we can't afford. What I am saying is that your state of mind is what makes your retirement good or bad." According to a 68-year-old widow, who reports a $15,000 income: "The main drawback of retirement for me is the fact that while my financial situation is not meager, and I am living pretty much on the same level as I did formerly, there is, nevertheless, a difference between now and before retirement. While I was working, my salary, together with my husband's, allowed for more than maintaining a certain standard of living. There was money left for travel, and a new car when needed. Today, my traveling has been considerably curtailed and the need for a new car can be a problem."

A 78-year-old man, with $30,000 in income, says: "A main attraction of retirement supposedly is being able to do what we want to do, yet we too often find our funds too slender for all of that." And a 72-year-old married woman, with an income of $50,000, writes, "My husband and I were able to participate in TIAA only late in our careers — as librarians we were only accorded faculty status fairly recently. We knew we must plan for our own financial security and believe we have been successful. Some of our expectations have been achieved, but with the inflation which increased costs enormously, and for which the retiree cannot hope to gain a share of increased income to match current and recent price increases, we have had to exercise care in our expenditures."

INCIDENTALLY: INCOME AND STANDARD OF LIVING

Our retirees' replies to questions about their financial status are generally reassuring, particularly in light of the inflation and turbulent economic conditions in the years preceeding the survey.

When asked, "How well would you say you are living, considering both income and expenses?", half checked off the answer categories "very well" or "well," and slightly less than a third checked "adequately." Only a handful said they are living "not too well." The survey also asked, "Compared to when you retired, how do you feel your overall financial situation in general is now— better, worse, or about the same?" Almost 30% feel their financial situation is better, half believe it's about the same, and about 15% think it's worse.

In addition, we asked our retirees to estimate the extent to which their total retirement income replaces their working-years income on a nominal basis, that is, unadjusted for the purchasing power loss caused by inflation since the individuals retired. Half estimate their current income is more than (25%) or about the same as (25%) their income before they retired. Another 25% of the retirees report their retirement income replaces from two-thirds to over three-quarters of their pre-retirement income. Only about 10% say their current income is less than half their pre-retirement income.

Slightly more than a quarter of the retirees had total annual household 1981 incomes, including income of spouses, of under $15,000, about a quarter had incomes between $15,000 and $25,000, another quarter have incomes between $25,000 and $40,000, and slightly less than a quarter had incomes of more than $40,000. Retirees with low incomes include a high proportion of women, not-marrieds, and former support staff personnel, while those with high incomes tend to be men, married, and former faculty and academic administrators.

When looked at by age, older retirees generally have lower incomes than younger retirees. A significant reason for the difference is former salary level — salaries in the 1930s, 1940s, and 1950s were much lower than those in the 1960s and 1970s. Although older retirees generally have lower incomes, they don't see themselves as financially deprived in comparison to younger, more recent retirees. Partly, this is because their present incomes are not perceived as small in the perspective of their lifetime salary history. Also, of course, everyone eventually adjusts to their income level, no matter what the level may be, as long as it does not drop drastically.

Many retirees urge people to save on their own for retirement during the working years in order to produce retirement income over and above pension and Social Security income. The extra income, their comments indicate, will not only minimize the financial adjustments retirees experience but, perhaps more importantly, can be a powerful tool to shape retirees' quality of life. Income helps determine the flexibility a retiree has to choose a retirement lifestyle; the higher the income, the greater the options. "To keep the style of living you've had in the past," suggests a 65-year-old woman with household income of $30,000, "save some money and have sufficient income. Therefore, make your preparations well in advance." She retired when her husband did and has since returned to work as a dental secretary in order to earn added income. Adds a 66-year-old man, with income of $25,000 and different goals for his income, "I'd pay more attention to financial preparations. Not that I'm in financial pain, but I could support worthy causes more generously."

Financial flexibility enabled a 62-year-old man, with income of $35,000, to shape the transition into retirement in his own way. He writes: "I retired from a TIAA arrangement made with a previous employer. I took early retirement in order that I could move to California to be near daughter and grandchildren. Retirement income permitted me to accept a job of lesser responsibility and pay. This provided a 'slow down' rather than a 'shut down' of my professional activities. At age 65 I plan to arrange another step-down by taking Social Security and starting a small self-employment business in my profession. Someday I may quit entirely but not while I have good health."

In addition to financing the expected expenses of everyday retirement, an adequate level of retirement income and savings is useful to help weather the consequences of the unexpected. As alluded to in an earlier comment, these include economic forces, such as inflation. According to a 72-year-old former teacher in a private secondary school, with an income of $25,000: "I have been a miser all my life and am glad about it since without my savings I would be in straitened circumstances due to the unexpectedly high rate of inflation." Another major concern of our retirees is that the unforseen costs of treating a major illness can wipe out their savings. According to a 63-year-old man with a $12,500 income: "More than half of my income at present is being used to pay for hospital, doctor, and medication, due to unexpected illness immediately following my retirement. Not complaining though. Just trying to make the best of it."

Certain kinds of unexpected family problems can also deplete retirement assets. A 63-year-old man with a $40,000 income, for example, notes how: "Personal planning by retiree and spouse was adequate and put into operation. However, actions beyond our control — death and/or divorce of children — can and do adversely affect the physical and financial capabilities of retired persons." And a 61-year-old woman, with an income of $25,000 and who "was under the impression that I was financially secure," had to deal with the loss of a large portion of her family's savings when her son's business failed three months after she retired at the age of 58. Because Social Security payments in her case cannot start until age 62 (at the earliest) she has had to return to work, but her enthusiasm in general, and for retirement in particular, isn't dampened. She writes: "I believe retirement years can be the best years of our lives if we are blessed with health and financial security. It will be rewarding to the extent that I make it so attitudinally. I firmly believe those later years after a lifetime of work and responsibility can be delightful! I can't wait until, at 62 or 65, I can say good-by to the pressures and demands of my work situation and pursue other interests."

The extent of our retirees' financial planning varied. At one extreme is a 66-year-old man with income of $25,000 who writes: "One never has enough funds, so I guess I would have tried harder to have made more money. But hell! I figured I'd rather enjoy what I had than die making what I couldn't use. I think my wife and I did as well as we could have — it was planned well enough in general, not in minute detail, and we were at the age to roll with the punches as they developed. We feel, for example, we have had the resources to provide adequately for our health needs, physically and mentally— this can be a big fat worry."

At the other extreme, some retirees attempted to develop retirement-oriented household budgets for their new lifestyles. Working up a new budget could reveal, for example, that the cost of a favorite retirement activity could consume the cost savings expected from ending certain work-related activities, such as commuting to work. Suggests a 77-year-old man, with income of $25,000: "Make an adequate and realistic postretirement analysis of income and budget. The travel and recreational activity I had anticipated had to be drastically revised." Some retirees engaged in particularly detailed financial planning. The long *Essay* — "It Took Some Self-Discipline" — written by a 69-year-old with a $30,000 retirement income provides a particularly penetrating look at how one couple planned.

ESSAY: "IT TOOK SOME SELF-DISCIPLINE"

Let me use this space to say something about some financial planning that seems to have worked. Twenty or more years before retirement I realized that I would not have the retirement income that I would need to be comfortable, and I started two related plans:

(1) The first plan concerned ordinary living, without the "extras." My wife and I decided that we would live on my basic income, after taxes and deductions for TIAA-CREF and Social Security. We used the best available projections of retirement income from these sources, after taxes, and compared this with current income after taxes and deductions. The figures fell a little short and there was nothing we could do about it at the time. As the years passed and my income increased, I put part of the increase (after increased taxes and deductions) into additional contributions to CREF and made new projections comparing available retirement income with current available income.

After the children finished college and were married, and after the house was paid for, we did not increase our spending, but put the money that had gone for children and house (principal and interest) into greater contributions to CREF. I continued comparing projected income after retirement with current available income, and adjusted the increased contributions to make these match as closely as I could.

It worked! My available income after retirement (TIAA, CREF, and Social Security, minus taxes) was very close to the available income before retirement (base income minus taxes and retirement contributions). I have depended on periodic increases in annuities and Social Security to take care of increases in the cost of living owing to inflation. Note that this plan did not allow for extras such as trips, a new car, etc. before retirement, and does not allow for these after retirement. These are taken care of in part two of the plan.

(2) The second plan is for the extras, and it took some self-discipline that wasn't always easy. This was the use of extra income, whether it was from summer teaching, consulting, writing, or my wife working. We figured the income taxes on this income by placing it on "top," at the top level for income taxes. Everything that was left was divided into two (later three) parts. One half was used for the extras that we enjoy, such as a trip or a new car, and the other half was invested, mostly in growth stocks (with a few mistakes).

If we wanted a new car or a special vacation trip, we had to work for it and realize that only a part of the additional earnings could be used. All investment dividends and gains (after taxes) were reinvested. There were a few emergencies that required extra funds, and we borrowed from ourselves for these, and paid ourselves interest. The only exception was when we built a new home three years before retirement, and didn't have quite enough to make it just what we wanted. At that point we divided the extra income after taxes into thirds, used two of these parts as we had before and put the third part into the new house. We also had to borrow from ourselves to have the extra niceties we wanted in the house, and don't see how we can repay ourselves, but this isn't hurting and we think it is worth sacrificing a trip or so.

Now that I am retired, the fund built up by this second plan has been reinvested, gradually, into income-producing securities and we spend part of that income (after taxes) on travel and an occasional new car. My wife is still working, part-time, and her income is treated as an extra, the way we did for more than 20 years. She pays the taxes, puts the maximum allowable into an IRA, and the remainder is divided into two parts—one part for her investments and one part for trips and a new car. When she retires in a few years, her IRA income and investment income will replace the part of her current earnings we now use for extras.

I've gone into some detail on this, and I hope it will suggest similar pre-retirement planning for some others. We slid into retirement with no change in our style of living, except perhaps an extra trip or so.

— 69-year-old married man

While many retirees agree that pre-retirement financial planning is important, they also recognize the practical difficulties that have to be overcome to carry out a financial plan. One hurdle, they say, is the natural concentration on the here-and-now. In the words of a 68-year-old man with an income of $35,000: "The only thing I might do differently is to start a sensible, safe investment plan sooner. But when one is young, it is inconceivable that he should grow old and die." "At age 18," asks a 67-year-old woman with an income of $25,000, "who thinks of retirement?" In a variation of this theme, a 66-year-old man, with an income of $20,000, says, "I should have looked into investment of earnings starting with the day I first became employed. However, I was more interested in my work."

There are other complications, of course, like the temptation to divert retirement savings to emergency uses during the working years. However, tapping one's retirement fund this way may not be prudent in a longer-term context. For example, a 71-year-old man with $20,000 in income writes: "If I could have matured just a bit sooner in life or foreseen the future just a bit better, I would have realized the importance of planning my finances better and paid more attention to building up my retirement funds. Twice, on different jobs, I drew out retirement funds in earlier years for some temporary 'important' need of the time. I should not have done that."

Saving for retirement is understandably difficult for people who have low-paying jobs. A former worker in a college infirmary, with an income of $7,500, says, "I never was able to save any money for retirement as my pay wasn't much. Now I feel the cost of living is so great that I can't do all I would like to do. That's why I would like a little job, for my own spending money, two or three days a week." A 70-year-old widow with an income of $10,000 writes that, "I couldn't build much retirement at the university working at the laundry. I had to work for such a small wage the first 14 years that I didn't build much retirement and therefore am only drawing $181 a month, which certainly does not buy much these days. My Social Security isn't much, so I have to live with my daughter to stretch my money for eating and a roof over my head, and surely there's no money for much recreation." Even people with higher retirement incomes make similar points. For example, a 68-year-old man with a $20,000 retirement income notes, "I wish I had entered TIAA-CREF at the very onset, but I felt I was earning too little to have the extra deductions." In other cases, retirees had priorities for their income other than building up retirement savings. "We wish we had more money put aside and invested earlier in life, but feel three children came first," says a 64-year-old woman with a $20,000 retirement income. A 75-year-old widower with a $25,000 retirement income adds, "One could say I should have saved and planned more for my retirement years, but my answer is that we had to live and enjoy during our working days."

Some retirees write that lack of information is a significant obstacle to adequate financial planning. For example, a 72-year-old single woman who did not reveal her income writes: "If I had been told by my employer that I could have matched what was paid by the college, my retirement income would have been much more. I am ashamed to tell anyone of what little I get with 40 years of service. I just hope the younger ones now will be better informed, so when they reach retirement age their retirement will mean something to them."

An information gap for other retirees, often mentioned by widows and single women in particular, was a general lack of knowledge about financial matters. Says a 72-year-old widow, a former college placement director who did not reveal her income range, "I wish I had learned more about handling my financial affairs or had found an advisor I could trust." Adds another widow in her 70s, with a $10,000 income, "I wish there had been as much information and emphasis on money management during my early working years so that I might have built up more individual retirement security." A 69-year-old widow, also with a $10,000 retirement income, says: "I should have learned more about economics in order to have accumulated a better retirement fund. Otherwise it's fun being retired and living each day to the fullest." The need for some self-sufficiency when it comes to understanding financial matters isn't limited to widows and single women, however. Others recognize they could or should have become more knowledgeable in the sense that they should have evaluated the "experts" with more care. Complains a 75-year-old man with a $50,000 income: "If I had it to do over again, I would have made better informed investments in the stock market, being more skeptical about my broker's recommendations."

Many did save successfully, such as an 82-year-old woman who taught public adult school classes for foreign students and who reports a household retirement income of $50,000. She writes: "When my husband was young, he read a bit of advice to the effect that everyone has an *extra* person to provide for— his older self. He began planning for retirement early." For most of us, accumulating a suitable level of retirement income is a long-term proposition simply because we need time to take advantage of the cumulative effect of regular savings and the power of compounding of earnings on those savings. (Since numbers make these points most tellingly, we developed some examples of the effect of long-term saving. See the discussion, "How Time (And the Tax Laws) Can Help the Retirement Saver," at the end of this chapter.) "At a very early age, endowed with my present wisdom, I would have saved more, much more, so that the simple fact of compound interest would have provided for an uncomplicated financial future," says a 63-year-old man with a $25,000 retirement income. Adds a 67-year-old man, formerly on the technical staff of a research organization, with a $30,000 retirement income: "It will be necessary in the future for very young people early in their careers— say age 25 or even at 20— to start saving at a small rate, but constantly, for a good retirement income when they need it. Over the years, it is surprising how a small but constantly deposited amount becomes so large."

COMMENTS: ON MONEY

HOUSEHOLD INCOME OF $10,000 OR LESS

If I were in a position to plan differently as to finances, I think that I should increase the savings rate, which would mean, mainly, reducing vacation travel expense each year.

—*86-year-old married man*

I would have tried to save more money on a retirement plan basis. It is a big adjustment you have to make in your life after retirement, financially and otherwise.

—*76-year-old widow*

One thing that could be done is to put more stress on saving, *much* earlier, so that more emphasis would be on taking care of oneself. I had the notion that Social Security plus the retirement policy would be more than they are, and certainly the great increase in expense which we have seen in the last few years has cut deeply into the income I thought I would have. The income is OK. The expense is terrific.

—*77-year-old married woman*

I would definitely have saved more money. I think the IRA plans available today make a lot of sense. If they were offered when I was working, I definitely would have invested in one.

—*76-year-old widow*

It seems that about the only attraction of my retirement is that we have a very *modest* but comfortable little home that is free from debt and a decent car, and we are free to come and go at will. The main drawback is that we do not have money enough or good enough health to go very far. I am very thankful to be able to take care of myself and still able to be "on foot" and that we have enough income to stay out of debt. Had I known I was going to have problems with my health, I would have tried to have saved a little more of my income. The pay for the job I was doing has more than doubled since I took my leave of absence, and I surely wish I could have stayed on and earned the wages they are earning on that job now.

—*66-year-old married woman*

HOUSEHOLD INCOME BETWEEN $10,000 AND $20,000

At least by age 30 establish some kind of retirement fund. Better yet, get a job where you are automatically enrolled from day one in a good retirement program.

—*63-year-old widow*

Should have gotten into TIAA-CREF a lot sooner, which would show it on my monthly checks now. Just never thought I could afford it I guess.

— 68-year-old married man

I recall that at the time of my joining— by compulsion— TIAA-CREF, I resented the deduction from my salary. Now I wish it had been more, much more. I feel that pre-retirees, especially those in small private schools, need someone to educate them on financial matters: stocks and bonds, investment in mutual funds, etc. This I consider of prime importance. My income is small, but I live quite happily and manage to save something.

— 84-year-old widow

I think I would have started to save something each month at a younger age than I did, so that I would have a little more *mad money.*

— 70-year-old single woman

I would have made more effort to invest money. It is important to start early and stick with it.

— 68-year-old married woman

I, like so many, many younger people, couldn't do without another weekly six-pack or, instead of eating out I could have stayed home for dinner on a few weekends *and* invested that much more per week in TIAA-CREF — which at this stage of the game would have meant quite a substantial sum extra.

— 66-year-old married man

If I were to do it again, I would have insisted that my four children pay half the cost of their college education. I paid all of it. Then I would take that $40,000, invest it, and retire 5 years earlier.

— 65-year-old married man

INCOME BETWEEN $20,000 AND $30,000

It would have been good to have put more money into annuities but that really wasn't possible on a modest income and still give our children college educations. In some ways, I think perhaps it is easier for people with modest lifetime incomes to adjust to retirement than for the more affluent.

— 65-year-old married woman

It would have helped if I had received more complete information at the time my university adopted the TIAA-CREF retirement plan. I didn't receive sufficiently adequate information to appraise the advantages and disadvantages of joining TIAA-CREF compared to continuing the non-contributory retirement program which was being phased out but continued for those who believed it was to their advantage to remain under it. Later, salaries increased substantially and the university contributions to TIAA-CREF for individual faculty members were greatly increased while the university contributions for faculty in the non-contributory program remained essentially the same. So I made a mistake not to join TIAA-CREF. Also, I should have started my personal tax-deferred annuity program with TIAA much earlier, but again the advantages were not adequately pointed out to me.

—72-year-old married man

The main drawback of retirement is that you have to stick to a good budget; the amount of money coming in is all there is. When working, there is some overtime and so you have some extra money coming in from time to time.

—63-year-old married man

Freedom says it all. I really enjoy my retirement! The main drawback is the constraint that you have to exert in your spending (because of lack of funds).

—63-year-old married man

INCOME BETWEEN $30,000 AND $40,000

To allow for such factors as inflation and out of consideration for the surviving husband or wife, I believe it is essential that any married couple make plans before retirement for some sort of retirement income in addition to those from TIAA-CREF, etc., and Social Security. This could be through a post-retirement part-time job, a business venture, rental property, or investment in securities paying dividends or interest. As one grows older it will become increasingly difficult to hold a job or manage a business or rental property, so investments in securities would be in most cases the most desirable of these alternate sources of income.

—68-year-old married man

Except for three years, I taught in private schools which did not have adequate pension plans. I enjoyed this teaching but it did not prepare me for retirement. I might have chosen schools with adequate pension systems, but my marriage made this unnecessary.

—85-year-old married woman

I would certainly have tried to manage my finances so that saving for retirement would have started when in my 30s and would have made certain that insurance was provided for my wife. I would have investigated a number of places for retirement living to make certain of more advantages than a good climate, and especially to have known more as to living expenses. On investments after retirement, more care should have been exercised to insure the safety against loss, especially of principal.

—71-year-old married man

I reduced my "wants" long ago, particularly about "conspicuous consumption," e.g., camper is 19 years old; small car is 12 years old; house and furniture old; etc. That attitude helps to make the adjustments to retirement— except for the travel bug.

—66-year-old married woman

Get more money to procure a better cello and buy more books.

—71-year-old married man

Regardless of the sacrifice (a simple example would be taking lunch and drink to work each day) I had a small sum taken automatically from my cheque each month and placed in my savings. What one can accumulate over the years will prove astounding.

—73-year-old married woman

I'm not typical in that I inherited a substantial amount of money when I was 65. If I were dependent on my pension, Social Security, and income from my own savings, I would still be living adequately and enjoying retirement, but I wouldn't be able to travel as much as I have, and I'd have to think twice about buying tickets for concerts and theater, eating out, etc. I'm finding retirement so satisfying that I can't think of anything that could make it more rewarding. However, if I hadn't inherited that money, I'm sure I would now be wishing I had started saving for retirement earlier and more regularly— though at the time it never seemed as if there was money available for saving.

—68-year-old single woman

INCOME MORE THAN $40,000

We would have begun our program of property acquisition much sooner than we did and I believe we would have diversified earlier and, perhaps, more successfully. We would also have begun our publishing venture sooner and developed a broader line of materials. However, we started earlier than many and really have no complaint with our preparations for retirement. We knew we could not live on income from the several retirement programs by which we were covered and so we prepared alternate sources of income, set a retirement date, and met it.

—65-year-old married man

I am fortunate enough to have an income that enables me to do what I want (within reason). My preretirement plans did include specific work and planning to make as sure as possible that I would have a fair financial freedom. However, so many retirees have a very limited financial program and therefore have a very restricted life after retirement — and are unhappy about being retired.

I have had many friends who worried two or three years prior to retirement that they would not have enough money to get along on when retired. Yet most found that they did in fact have adequate financial means when retired. Preretirement counseling should emphasize the "money side" of being retired. So many worry saying "I spend my whole salary now when I'm working — how am I going to make out on a one-half retirement?" My observation of retired teacher friends is that with Social Security, TIAA-CREF, investment income, etc., they find out that they make it OK. Most say that the main problem is buying a new car. So counseling should try to guide pre-retirees in developing as sound a retirement nestegg as possible — and to appreciate the fact that they can get along fairly well in retirement.

—74-year-old married man

(1) Retirement provides freedom for a person to pursue his interests, provided he has been fortunate enough to have been blessed with average or better health. Financial planning over a lifetime is essential to enjoy this freedom.

(2) There is no set pattern which could be prescribed for all because each individual varies too greatly in background, interests, physical and mental health, and financial status at the time of retirement. Most people, however, will enjoy these years more if they have planned far enough in advance to give them financial freedom.

(3) Health and adequate finances are two of the most important ingredients. Given these, an inventory of one's interests should aid in planning an enjoyable retirement life. Without these, some may find retirement a most unhappy period.

—74-year-old married man

I wish I could have contributed more money to my TIAA-CREF retirement program during the 18 years I was with the program so that my benefits would be more substantial.

—65-year-old married woman

If I had it to do over, I would put more money into retirement. This would have meant living on a reduced scale, but I think it would be well worth it. Aside from financial concerns, I have no other changes I would make. I am able to do all the things that I didn't have time for while working and I have many interests to which I am now devoting more and more time.

—64-year-old married man

Concern About Inflation And Social Security

Only about a third of the retirees checked "yes" in answer to the question, "Since you retired, have you had to make any adjustments in your lifestyle because of increases in the cost of living?" The other two-thirds checked off "no." Several factors may account for this surprising finding. For example, retirees were insulated from cost of living increases to some extent during the 1970s: Social Security benefits were indexed to increases in the Consumer Price Index and, following the introduction of money market mutual funds and the lifting of interest rate controls on bank deposits, savings interest rates could more closely keep pace with inflation. Also, at the time of the survey, in late 1982, the rate of inflation had begun to moderate after several years of extremely high increases.

Of those who did make adjustments, inflation affected some more than others. Cutbacks ranged from travel, vacations, dining out, and entertainment, to clothes and other "basics." Says a 70-year-old woman, "Medical bills and fuel costs have eaten up all extra money— that and the very real needs of our children." And a 75-year-old widower writes, "The present inflation and the threat of even greater inflation has forced me to keep a watchful eye — more than normal or comfortable — on my spending for necessities and recreational activities."

Retirees at all income levels worry about income adequacy in inflationary times but, as you might expect, those with low incomes report having been particularly hard hit. "Things skyrocketed when I retired and stop me on every hand from doing my thing," says a 64-year-old widow who says her income is $5,000. "Needless to say, in the light of inflation, I should have done more saving," says an 80-year-old widow with income of $12,500. "Perhaps I geared my thinking to magazine ads from many years ago that pictured an elderly couple with the caption 'How we retired on $300 a month.' What dreamers many of us were!" A 68-year-old married man, with income of $35,000, tells of "concern over inflation, but for the near future we are satisfied, and have not had to draw down our savings."

The severe inflation of the late-1970s and early-1980s makes some retirees worry about future rates of inflation. "Unless inflation can be totally stabilized, which is most unlikely," says a 73-year-old man with income of $50,000, "the retiree always must fear the future and hope he doesn't live *too* long." Complains a 79-year-old man, who reports a $40,000 income, "The last 10 years of economic trends were not considered in faculty discussions about retirement plans 40 years ago. And what discussions go on presently are probably no more tuned to 2020 payouts than our discussions in 1940 were tuned to 1982."

Social Security is the principal income source for the majority of the retirees, and many are concerned about whether their Social Security income will continue to keep pace with rising living costs. This question was particularly prominent at the time of our survey because considerable national attention was then being given to the financial plight of the Social Security system. "There is an *insecurity financially* by being dependent on income from Social Security (will it continue?) and interest/dividends (affected by our economy). One defers an expensive trip to save the money, etc.," says a 65-year-old woman, with income of $20,000.

An 80-year-old woman, whose income is $5,000, has apparently been well-served by the Social Security program and, understandably, is concerned about it. She says: "I am very well satisfied with my retirement. We paid for our home and cars and land before retirement and never ran credit of any kind since that time. I remember how it was with my parents. There was no retirement for them and no money to live on when they could no longer work. I'm so thankful for Social Security and so afraid the government may cut it back or take it away from us. We need more Medicare for eye care, ears, and dental work."

According to a 79-year-old man, with a $25,000 income: "We have saved for retirement as much as we could spare. After we raised two sons, the mother was able to take a teaching position until retirement age, allowing us to put away some savings and to qualify for two Social Security incomes. Without this Social Security and our thrift, we would be in difficult straits."

INCIDENTALLY: HOW TIME (AND THE TAX LAWS) CAN HELP THE RETIREMENT SAVER

Some numerical examples might help explain why some of our retirees say that the sooner one begins saving the better.

Let's start with compound interest. A one-time deposit, no matter what the amount, earning 10% annual interest grows to 2½ times the original amount over 10 years because interest is earned on interest as well as on the deposit. More typically, however, people save on a regular basis, and this kind of saver also benefits from earning interest on interest. For example, saving $100 a month for 10 years at a 10% compound interest rate produces a final savings amount of nearly $21,000.

The power of compound interest and constant savings, however, can be weakened by taxes. Assuming a 30% tax bracket, the saver in the above example had to earn $143 a month in order to have $100 a month to set aside as savings after taxes are paid. Taking taxes into account also means that the saver is not earning a full 10%, but is effectively earning 7%. Under these conditions, the 10-year-saver's accumulation, after taxes are paid on the interest, comes to about $17,500 — less than the no-tax example.

Any saver, of course, can take advantage of the power of compound interest and regular saving. Retirement savers also have the opportunity to use another technique that can add appreciably to their retirement funds — tax deferral.

Some retirement savings opportunities, such as Individual Retirement Accounts and certain types of tax-deferred annuities, allow (continuing with our example above) the full pre-tax $143 to be set aside as retirement savings with no taxes paid at that time. Saving $143 a month rather than $100 significantly adds to the buildup of savings *without affecting take-home pay.* Moreover, taxes on the earnings from tax-deferred savings are also deferred.

Whatever retirement savings vehicle is used, the end-result of all these factors working together for the saver — compounding, regular savings, tax-deferral— can be impressive. To illustrate: the person in our example, saving $143 a month (before taxes are deducted from pay) at a 10% compound annual interest rate (on which taxes are deferred) would accumulate almost $30,000 in a decade— 70% more than through non-tax-deferred savings. The result of saving longer would be even more impressive. For example, over 20 years that accumulation would be $109,500— *double* the amount that would be accumulated on a non-tax-deferral basis.

Of course, taxes eventually have to be paid on tax-deferred savings when the saver receives the funds in retirement, although if the funds are withdrawn as a stream of income during the retirement years the income-boosting effect of tax-deferral and compounding continues for some time. One more wrinkle: The tax rate for most retirees is lower that their pre-retirement tax rate, and this means additional benefits to them from tax-deferral. Also, in all but a small minority of financial situations, tax-deferral is a worthwhile strategy for those whose tax rates are higher in retirement.

Chapter 9: AGING AND HEALTH

A Blessing That Money Can't Buy

Ninety percent of our retirees say they are comparatively healthy. We asked them to rate their health in relation to others their age, and 50% rate their health as "excellent" or "very good" compared to their chronological peers. Another 40% think their health is "good", and only about 10% describe themselves as in comparatively "poor" or "very poor" health. We also asked about the trend of their health in recent years: about three-quarters feel their health is "about the same" now as in recent years, or even better, while about a quarter say their health is "not as good now."

In the essay portion of our questionnaire, our retirees write that physical health is one of the two most critical factors (the other being financial health) shaping the retirement experience. If they had to rank the two factors, their comments suggest physical health is slightly more important— agreeing in various ways with the adage that good health is a blessing that money can't buy. "There is no comparison now between the value of muscle tone and the value of money," says a 78-year-old woman who wishes she had exercised more when she was younger. A 71-year-old man, in ill-health recently, observes: "If I could plan my retirement again, I'd plan to retire at 62, with less income and greater physical stamina. In my case, it would have been helpful to be jolted into an awareness that life is not really infinite, before a health problem forces that recognition. I just didn't open my eyes and see the truth."

Some retirees caution that retirement and old age should be kept in perspective. Certainly, they are coincident events for most of us. But retirement in and of itself does not mean an immediate and automatic decline in physical and mental vigor. As a 66-year-old woman notes, "The drawbacks that I am aware of are more those of 'aging' rather than 'retirement.'" A 79-year-old widower puts it this way: "The decrease in vitality, energy, and physical activity due to advancing age — and the mental and emotional effects thereof — *accompany* continued retirement but of course can't be *blamed on* retirement per se. Retirement enters in only by making it easier to adapt to one's new circumstances." Of course, age and health status should be taken into account when planning retirement activities. According to a 73-year-old man, who categorizes himself as in "very good" health: "One's physical health must be considered in the planning of your retirement years. A program of much activity to seek fulfillment of your dreams must be tempered by the possibility of physical and health problems. One must be prepared to accept the fact that whatever you do must be within the boundaries of your endurance."

As previous chapters on activities indicate, many of the retirees are quite active, reflecting to a large extent their generally good health status. The earlier years in particular can be an active period for most retirees. A 67-year-old man who retired at 65, for example, notes that "in the first 10 months of retirement, I ran my first marathon," and a 70-year-old widow says, "I find myself with abundant energy and ability to work some more. It begins to look like age 70 is not necessarily the right age for retirement for everyone." A 67-year-old woman describes her active schedule: "I find I have to discipline myself to keep a normal routine — get up by 7:30 or 8:00 a.m. and get to bed at a reasonable hour. I knew before I retired that I could easily turn night into day as I am a night person, so I have been careful to schedule my activities in order to maintain a normal schedule which results in no problem. While I have not personally experienced it, I resent the media referring to people retired in their 60s as elderly. Maybe at 75 or 80 years of age this category applies, but not to people younger. I planned carefully for retirement and my only regret is that there are not enough hours in the day to cover all my interests."

Active retirement can continue in the later years as well. An 80-year-old woman writes: "I worked for a salary for 50 years and now that I am doing volunteer work I like the freedom of choice I have as to days and hours of work. I hope to continue for a long time, for I am really a workaholic." An 80-year-old man offers this view: "I am busier than ever before. But the ability to do everything that I would like to undertake is diminished because of the weaknesses and restrictions that advancing years impose. But positive thinking has kept these drawbacks at bay, thank the Lord."

Indeed, some of our retirees use the questionnaire to scold those who view retired persons in stereotypes. "Some people treat seniors as if they're over the hill. It's tiresome to be gushed over," says a 72-year-old woman. According to a 67-year-old man, "Intelligent people meet retirement with the same fortitude, application, and insight they applied to preretirement circumstances. The presumption that upon retirement one immediately becomes senile and unable to act for himself is vastly misplaced. Common sense, well developed at retirement age, will sustain anyone."

A 90-year-old woman also took the opportunity to vent her frustration about younger people's perceptions. "Drawbacks in retirement are few," she writes. "I tire more easily and I need more sleep (which I get). I'm upset by conversation in large groups because I am deaf and my hearing aid only exaggerates the noise." But she adds: "Some people who mean to be kind in speaking to me are patronizing instead because they don't understand, or because they don't believe, that I am still fairly intelligent. That is carping, I know, but it is a relief to say it!"

Despite the comparative overall good health of many of our retirees, increasing age has had an effect on some individuals' physical condition, especially those over 75. "The first 10 years of retirement were for us personally splendid," says a 78-year-old man, who rates his and his 77-year-old wife's health as "excellent" despite some "deteriorations due to aging." It is "around age 75 or 76," he says, "that minor frailties and infirmities accumulate with all too much speed." To one 74-year-old man — who rates his health as "very poor" — added ailments and loss of energy are about the only significant drawbacks of retirement. "Drawbacks are due exclusively to deterioration of health during the last two years. Otherwise there are none," he writes.

A common complaint is a general decline in stamina. "The main drawback of retirement is I am getting older and slowing down," says a 67-year-old man, who sees himself as in "good" health. An 81-year-old man wishes: "I would have taken opportunities in vacations to travel where vigor is essential, and to sample accommodations with a view to post-retirement use, without the vigor of younger years. Unless one retires early enough, exploration becomes less and less appealing. I believe now that I should have retired earlier." At the same time, our retirees write that they welcome retirement as a way to adjust to their lower levels of stamina. Says a 72-year-old woman, "I can feel myself slowing up. I worked hard all my life. Now I feel like taking a nap in the afternoon."

In some cases, declining health — either retirees' or their spouses' — has derailed some retirement plans. For example, an 83-year-old man who rates his health as "poor" writes that: "I now would like to finish three or more publications on a scholarly basis but cannot leave the house to go to libraries because of the state of my wife's health. My own health is beginning to deteriorate, perhaps because of my life in retirement." And a wife who writes in for her 82-year-old husband says that: "He was very healthy in every way until he started, about the time he retired at age 70, to get Alzheimer's Disease. My husband has been in a nursing home for nearly five years. We were going to travel and he had great plans to do more research on Latin America and write another book."

Severe health problems have a social dimension as well — they can lead to loneliness as chances to socialize are curtailed. A 77-year-old woman chronicles a related problem: "As I have had both a stroke (1980) and a broken hip (1982), I have been much limited in my mobility, spend a lot of time sleeping, and am *bored* to tears part of the time. Before the stroke I went places and did things that I had wanted to do, like walking, going to the park, gardening, and visiting friends. I had intended to do some writing, but did not get much done — tomorrow, etc. — and now can write only a few letters, as my handwriting is not legible any more." Adds an 81-year-old woman, "A recent broken hip has made me dependent on friends for safe locomotion. My life has become dull, but with diminished energy I hardly want more."

In some cases, health problems have been carried into retirement from the working years. Some regret the strain they put themselves under during their working years and believe it had an effect on their health in retirement. "I was a workaholic and I overdid it," recalls a 72-year-old widower. "I enjoyed my work, was highly motivated, and felt that my efforts made an important contribution in my area of responsibility. During occasional periods of pressure or crisis I refused to compromise my standards. During one such unusually prolonged period, I suffered a mild heart attack which caused some permanent heart damage. It was followed six months later by a second and more frightening attack. It is possible that my health now would be better if I had paced myself more wisely or perhaps if I had accepted my doctor's advice to retire earlier." Adds a 63-year-old man, "I would have taken better care of my health in my earlier years. I took the job too seriously— few vacations, little time off, etc."

Some retirees mention another health concern that can influence one's life in a pervasive way — excessive drinking. The poignant *Essay* on the following page, "I Was Developing a Drinking Problem," describes the experiences of a 67-year-old man who seems to have conquered his alcoholism. The threat of alcoholism, this man cautions, is a very real one for retired people. He writes: "I have come to learn that late-blooming alcoholism, triggered in retirement by the removal of the restraints of employment, is a very common and a serious problem. I have met and counseled many others in my situation. Fortunately, alcoholism is treatable and controllable if there is an honest desire to do so. If I had it to do over again I would have sought alcohol counseling *before* retirement. Drinking problems will *not* clear themselves up automatically on retirement; they will, in fact, tend to get worse."

Many remain undaunted by physical and age limitations. A 78-year-old man, for example, explains how "I have worked hard on this questionnaire of yours, having been *suffering* an attack of shingles all of the past month." And a 77-year-old, who describes himself as "legally blind ever since there has been such a definition," describes some of his activities: "At age 76 I wrote a 250-page hard cover book for a state historical society and I made a gift of this book to the society. Much of my time is spent with talking books for the blind. I read from three to five books a week, mostly from 8 p.m. to 2 a.m. at night while lying in bed. I read everything, including some text books, and I have reread many of the classics many times." In addition, he says that he and his wife "spend much time writing letters to our children and grandchildren, trying our best to set a good example in letter writing and getting them to do likewise."

ESSAY: "I WAS DEVELOPING A DRINKING PROBLEM"

From early middle age I had planned to retire at age 60, and thanks to substantial investment income my plan was financially feasible. As that age approached my job-related stresses seemed to increase markedly. At the same time my consumption of alcohol also began to increase, rising above the modest levels of my earlier drinking pattern. In retrospect I see I was developing a drinking problem.

Although it was quite controllable, at that time it was nevertheless there and I did nothing about it. I assumed that the problem would disappear once I left the stresses of employment behind me. My wife and I had long wished to make a clean break with our environment on retirement. We planned to leave our many friends and our familiar and comfortable surroundings to seek a new life in a different part of the country. To this end we spent the five summers preceding retirement exploring various possibilities. Dismissing traditional retirement communities, we finally selected the small college town where we now live. We deliberately chose a region with a challenging seasonal climate and looked forward eagerly to our Great Adventure.

Our new environment was as totally stress-free as we had hoped. Congenial new friends were at hand and the social and intellectual life of the college was open to us. There were no financial problems. In short, as far as the externals were concerned, there were no surprises. In spite of this friendly environment, however, my consumption of alcohol, rather than decreasing as I had expected, began to increase substantially. My health began to suffer and a progressive deterioration of the spirit set in, extending over about a two-year period.

I finally came to realize that, relatively late in life, I had become an alcoholic. I sought treatment, joined Alcoholics Anonymous, and stopped drinking completely. Taking this step turned my life around in an amazing way. For the last five years I have been extremely active, productive, and — above all — happy. My health is better than it has been for 20 years. In short, life is now simply great.

— 67-year-old married man

An 85-year-old who had been very active — "I had been named Woman of the Year by two women's organizations," she notes — explains how: "I had reason to believe that I might have the opportunity to continue to serve in community affairs. I was disappointed. A very slight tremor has, with advancing years, become much more serious. Shortly after retirement I began refusing requests for appearances, which I could not make without embarrassment. My life is not unpleasant. My intimate friends understand and make allowances for my difficulty." Age and illness have not stopped a 79-year-old woman from being elected a Ruling Elder of her church at the age of 74 and actively serving in that post for three years. "That was one of the most satisfying experiences of my long life," she says, adding that, "I sometimes feel as though I am not a fully accepted member of society. This may be due to the fact that two years ago I fell and fractured one hip. After a long period of hospitalization due to complications I was just returning to normal when I fell again and broke the other hip! It has been a struggle to return to circulation and a normal (for me) life." Nevertheless, she continues: "I am also able to handle a large volume of correspondence. For the last few months I have been working on my memoirs, and am now ready to perfect the writing. My presumption for a satisfying retirement is to keep so busy there is little time for self-pity."

Many retirees rely on physical fitness activities to maintain a healthy physical status, such as the 63-year-old man who daily engages "in a lonely proposition of maintaining my health by an early morning walk-run," the 67-year-old who says, "each day I get up by 6:30 a.m. and go for an eight to ten mile bike ride, if the weather permmits," and the 76-year-old who rides 200 miles a month on his bike. Overall, a third of our retirees report they are participating in a sports or physical fitness program.

Others say exercise *would* have been a good idea (a notion that's common to younger people as well). "I regret having always thought myself too busy for exercise," says a 78-year-old woman. "If I were young now, or middle-aged, I wouldn't take up jogging. But golf if I could, or swimming, or Y exercise classes! That's it. Recommend yoga (not head-standing, but an Americanized yoga). That done from the 50s on should be good for the person, both then and later." Says a 70-year-old woman: "One thing I should have done was start and stick to a regular exercise program. Sometimes I get tired now and I wish I had a little more stamina." Adds a 67-year-old woman: "I should have started an exercise program before I retired so that I would be committed to a routine."

In summary, many of our retirees accept their health and aging as natural, as another phase of their lives that they must learn to adjust to. For example, an 84-year-old man who rates his health as "good" comments, "A drawback in retirement is physical limitations. You're not growing younger, but you can still live wisely so health can be maintained." And in the view of a 68-year-old who says he is in "very good" health: "There are drawbacks to growing old — one feels sick a lot and he sees his loved ones deteriorate in health. In a way it is sad, but it is nature's way and who can complain about that? I feel that I have made a meaningful contribution to life and that the world may be a bit better off because I have lived in it. Who could want anything more?"

COMMENTS: OBSERVATIONS ABOUT OLDER LIFE

The answer to a happy retirement is enough money, good health, and lots of nice people around!

—77-year-old single woman
(Rates health as comparatively "good")

I may have to reduce my lifestyle, especially overseas travel etc., some day. But chances are that some years hence, at an advanced age, I may not want (or be able) to travel to distant and exotic places (which involves substantial discomforts) as much as I have been doing.

The most important part of retirement is to remain active— I regularly engage in athletic activities, swim 50 laps every day, go hiking in the mountains most weekends and on vacations, and go skiing for several weeks each winter-spring, usually to the Alps. A few activities, such as weight lifting and running, I had to give up because of injuries which left permanent impairment. But I am happy with what I can do rather than make myself miserable thinking of what I can no longer do.

I also keep intellectually active, by keeping up my professional and general reading, and while I do much less writing than I used to do, I still accept offers to do pieces for publication or radio-TV and newspaper interviews, debates, etc. When I retired I thought I would now finally have enough time to organize my tens of thousands of color slides (33mm) and film (movies, mostly travel and mountain climbing), but now find that I have added many more and that they are not in better shape than they were seven years ago. In other words, I am always short of time and look forward to the day when I have time on my hands. That day may never come . . . .

—78-year-old divorced man
(Rates health as comparatively "excellent")

(1) Health problems have kept me from being as active professionally and socially as I would like to be. I am surprised and dismayed to find my general level of energy at 69 to be so much lower than five years ago. I have developed health problems that have continued to be difficult to diagnose and that have limited my activities. (From my personal experience, I wonder whether the present trend toward pushing retirement age to 70 may not cause difficulties for more people than is anticipated.)

I especially regret the limitation of professional activity that seems primarily related to these health problems. I have been fortunate in finding some interesting professional work (part paid and part volunteer) at a local museum that is directly related to some of my early anthropological work. However, I have not felt able to undertake the kind of projects that I had anticipated doing on my own in retirement.

(2) After 40 years in university teaching and research, I am aware that I work most productively in a structured situation, in which the demands of

the job help to set the routine and pace of work. I have found the unstructured environment of retirement more difficult to deal with than I had anticipated, and I suspect that this has intensified the barriers presented by my health problems.

(3) On a personal level, the distance from family and friends in the East is also a drawback. As we and they grow older, we find that travel is not as easy as it used to be, and I keenly regret the diminution or loss of these ties.

— 69-year-old married woman
(Rates health as comparatively "good")

I should have changed my doctor before retiring. The yearly ritual of a physical exam became just that. A new doctor could and should give a new and inquiring look and, hopefully, an educated finger pointing at developing problems.

— 71-year-old married man
(Rates health as comparatively "good")

Keep yourself busy. Don't give your mind time to think about your health or shortcomings. To do otherwise invites trouble.

— 68-year-old married man
(Rates health as comparatively "good")

We have both made a study of nutrition and have lost nearly 30 pounds each since my husband's retirement on July 1, 1980. Our doctor is delighted and so are we.

— 65-year-old married woman
(Rates health as comparatively "excellent")

Time for daily walks of about two miles. This activity, prescribed by my physician, is a great joy to me. It contributes to my health and it almost always brings some special added pleasure: the sight of the first pussy willow in spring, the chance encounter with a friend, the ever-changing beauty of nature, a glimpse of a happy child, a sandlot baseball game.

— 72-year-old widower
(Rates health as comparatively "poor")

We all have to be sensible about the fact that we all grow old and that there are various stages in our lives to which we must learn to adjust. I believe that I adjust quite easily, as I have been happy in all the stages of my life. I think God prepares us for every phase of life if we will let him, and when the time for retirement comes we find that we then have the time to find happiness if we just look for it among our friends and family.

— 79-year-old single woman
(Rates health as comparatively "good")

It is very pleasant to work in my vegetable garden and around my place; scout out a field trip for our Audubon group (which I established in the '50s); give a talk on some phase of gardening to our many garden groups in Florida; attend meetings of Nature Conservancy and Florida Audubon; take in reunions at my alma mater; visit some friend at a distance; etc. I keep busy enough in Florida in winter and the Carolinas in summer to enjoy life and not feel under pressure. I have enjoyed life and friends as I've gone along. Now have to ease up a bit and work slower.

— 86-year-old single woman
(Rates health as comparatively "very good")

(a) Freedom to undertake small projects and responsibilities at will with very moderate associated stress. (b) Time to exercise and relax as required for maximum health fitness.

— 73-year-old married man
(Rates health as comparatively "excellent")

Amazement at living so long and achieving greater perspective.

— 82-year-old married man
(Rates health as comparatively "good")

Attractions: Opportunities to engage in activities which are an end in themselves in terms of accomplishment and satisfaction. The satisfactions inherent in manual effort — the worth and pleasure of being physically tired at the end of a day.

— 67-year-old married man
(Rates health as comparatively "excellent")

A healthy preretirement lifestyle undoubtedly will pay high dividends.

— 64-year-old married woman
(Rates health as comparatively "very good")

Not only do we find our physical strength becoming weaker, our reaction times slower, and aches and pains increasing, but the senses somewhat impaired by the passing of the years. But the real danger, as I see it, is the attractiveness of becoming inactive and lazy and thus hastening the process of aging. It is too easy to sit in a comfortable chair and watch a television program that should never have been put on in the first place.

— 71-year-old married man
(Rates health as comparatively "good")

We keep very active and have a trailer in Canada for five months a year. We engage in a physical fitness program. We bicycle, swim, hike, and fish. We read a good deal. We travel and entertain more than before and attend more social functions. I still have not made up my mind if I will take more courses at college or do voluntary work.

—66-year-old married woman
(Rates health as comparatively "excellent")

I am living in a beautiful spot in Florida in a condominium. I have my own car and am able to drive "back north" about once a year. I am active in church, president of the Y.E.S. (Young Energetic Seniors) Group, and an officer in the Women's Society. The past 10 weeks I have worked as a volunteer in our Congressman's reelection campaign. My niece, who has two small children, lives nearby and I enjoy helping care for them. I have traveled quite a bit — Europe twice, Alaska, Greece, Egypt, and Israel, plus some USA trips. I took courses at a local community college, and enjoy reading and some TV programs. I swim in our pool and take long walks.

—74-year-old single woman
(Rates health as comparatively "excellent")

I greatly regret that many people view retired people as having diminished abilities, which is by no means necessarily true. I believe that many retirees who live separately from their families can show greater initiative, and so retain abilities that may be cramped and lessened either by supervision or by the view of family members that their capacities are inadequate for some activity or interest. And I regret the view that helplessness is a necessary aspect of aging. Aging is individual, and the person ought to be looked at individually, with understanding, and fairly. Many have continued to grow in their comprehension and even in their participation in daily life.

—82-year-old single woman
(Rates health as comparatively "excellent")

With my somewhat conspicuous physical limitations, I am far better off when I frankly allow younger people to help me. Sometimes I have even called upon strangers. To both friends and strangers this is evidently a pleasure — so why not accept their help for all that it's worth? I think that many elderly people suffer from excessive pride resulting in a denial of help which others find pleasure in giving.

—70-year-old single woman
(Rates health as comparatively "good")

Believe it or not, we have found no drawbacks! It may be a different story if we last to our upper 80s-early 90s, but I doubt it. As realists, we don't expect miracles, but we expect to be able to cope — unless senility be our lot!

—75-year-old married woman
(Rates health as comparatively "excellent")

ESSAY: "I CONTINUE TO MAKE AND FULFILL COMMITMENTS"

As before the retirement years — I retired in 1970 — I continue to make and fulfill commitments. Some activities are related to avocational interests (history, travel, Bible discussion). Other efforts are made toward achieving a hopeful outlook and direction in spite of concerns and problems.

My sister and I had 12 enjoyable years together, living in a two bedroom (two baths) apartment where there could be privacy yet social activities together and with friends. We have kept in contact with our friends and made new friends. We purchased memberships which opened up new opportunities for learning — Friends of Libraries (public, state, genealogy, international), art museum (includes music), Public Broadcasting (PBS). We have worked at the challenges of investing (one bankruptcy 1982), car buying (1979), record-keeping and filling out tax forms (using free advisory help), meeting health problems (each of us had a surgical problem in the 1970s), and of budgeting and spending.

My sister and I moved to this life-care facility in 1981. Understanding our life-care contract before moving into this facility and paying our endowment fee called for research and reading and asking questions of those individuals who had the information, and this made us understand what services are included in our monthly fee and those that are provided at no cost, and the reasons for increases of the monthly payment and guest meal costs. With the death of my sister, days have been filled with many different responsibilities. My brother and wife (who moved here last December because they needed medical services) and their children have been very supportive to me in my bereavement.

I continue to make and fulfill commitments. As executrix of my sister's will I am now working with a lawyer and also carrying out some of the contacts and duties on my own. I will continue learning — Elderhostel courses, TV classroom courses, and selected, informative presentations on stage and PBS. I will continue to seek and be with people who discuss/share ideas in small groups — who have a sense of humor — where we can laugh together, too.

— 74-year-old single woman

Health Insurance and Medical Costs

While money cannot buy health, money can buy health insurance. Our retirees are concerned about the costs of medical care and, in particular, the consequences of a catastrophic illness. "I don't think any of us retired folk fully realized the importance and magnitude of *health* in our later years. Mainly, the threat, emotionally and financially, of major or possibly terminal illness. The real possibility of a financial wipe-out is scary," notes a 60-year-old man. Some wish they had emergency savings available for major medical expenses. "If financial benefits available now were available to me while employed, I would take advantage of the savings plans to ward off the fear of expenses in a serious illness," says a 68-year-old woman.

Not surprisingly, almost all of the retirees have some health insurance. Our survey found that everyone over age 65 participates in the federal Medicare program — three-quarters in both Part A and Part B — and 90% of them have some form of medical expense insurance in addition to Medicare. Still, some express concern about the adequacy of their overall health insurance coverage.

Our retirees' comments strongly suggest that prospective retirees should make sure they understand the extent of the health insurance coverage they will have in retirement. The health insurance of some of our retirees ended at retirement, and occasionally this was unexpected. For example, a frustrated 73-year-old complains how "one discovers upon entering retirement that benefits such as group life insurance, health insurance, dental care, group purchasing plans, and others are instantaneously withdrawn. At a time when these benefits are perhaps most needed, they either are not available or they are offered at high cost." Some, such as this 68-year-old widow, realize they should have taken the initiative to better understand the extent of their insurance coverage. "I left too much to my husband's judgment," she says, and writes about "insufficient medical coverage provided by employers — Major Medical insurance terminated with retirement, both for spouse and self. Astronomical medical expenses of spouse inadequately covered."

Some retirees have decided to meet their health care needs by moving to a retirement life-care facility, where, along with housing, one is guaranteed medical care throughout old age. This possibility worked out well for a 73-year-old woman: "I planned so that I am now living in a wonderful retirement community which provides medical care in case of illness. This is near where I was born and grew up and so it was like coming home when I moved here nine years ago."

COMMENTS: CONCERN OVER MEDICAL COSTS

The process of filing claims has been time-consuming and aggravating. Without Medicare I would have been unable to handle the financial problems involved. My retirement income is not large enough for me to go to a nursing home or retirement community, which requires a large investment of funds.

— 79-year-old single woman

Drawbacks are primarily financial: Concern over the economy and its effect on my limited, fixed income. Concern over how to be prepared to meet spiraling hospital, medical, and dental costs as the need to incur them becomes greater each year, and especially when the benefits I was granted when working did not include some enjoyed today by many employees, such as dental insurance.

— 67-year-old single woman

If I had better health everything would be OK. The main drawbacks of retirement are that the cost of living keeps going up, the money that you do get has to go a longer way, and there's never enough. As you know, Medicare and health insurance do not pay for all of your doctor and hospital stays.

— 71-year-old married man

The hospitalization plans are strictly for the birds. I pay an exorbitant amount of money to be covered and I still have to make an initial payment to the doctor to activate the coverage.

— 76-year-old widow

Our retirement picture changed drastically. We had no Medicare at the time of my husband's four-year illness. This altered our carefully drawn retirement financial structure. I have since become trapped in spiraling prices of everything, but especially of medical fees, since Medicare gives inadequate coverage. I believe doctors should be willing to accept what Medicare allows. It might save the system and save some of us!

— 71-year-old widow

A word about Major Medical insurance and how it has worked in our recent experience: we have, through my employer university, a Major Medical plan with one of the largest insurance companies designed to pay for medical costs beyond those paid by Medicare (known as Medigap insurance). Our total medical expenses during the past year approximate $40,000, representing the costs of two major operations for my wife, two months in the hospital, plus some minor operations.

Medicare has supported these expenses very well, but our experience with claims presented to our Medigap insurer is far from satisfactory. Their office staff work was abominable. They lost claims and physicians' statements, paid claims directly to surgeons who had already been paid in full, etc., etc. What we did receive from the insurance company was paid with great reluctance, and only after I demanded a complete review of my claims (22 separate suppliers) by one competent auditor. Better Major Medical insurance to back Medicare is evidently needed by retired persons.

— 78-year-old married man

Have not been able to get Major Medical at any reasonable rate.

— 69-year-old widow

I hope I have more health insurance coverage than I shall ever need.

— 76-year-old single woman

Chapter 10: WHERE TO LIVE

Move Or Stay?

Three out of four of our retirees own their house, condominium, or co-op unit, and most of the rest rent. The majority live in the same home as before retirement; a substantial minority, however, relocated at or after retiring.

Among the retirees who stayed in their pre-retirement locales was a 76-year-old widow, who writes: "I have deep roots. I live in a town of 10,000, where I spent most of the year except for the three or four months (during the cold winter) that I spend in California. I have lived in my town for 44 years and I taught in the college 33 years, so I am well acquainted with many people in town who are very close friends. We have many cultural advantages and are within 60 miles of a larger city, which allows us to take advantage of its offerings as well."

A 76-year-old man and his wife also stayed in their long-time home. Says he: "We are quite contented in our house. I enjoy my association with the faculty and administration at my university. We have a nice house on a 2.2 acre lot near the bay. We go away in the summer for a few weeks just to get away from the telephone and the press of social and community obligations." And an 83-year-old widower comments: "We had lived on a farm nine miles from the university I worked at for 20 years before retirement. So I was kept busy (milked a cow for 18 years — not same cow) on farm before retirement and afterward. We actually built a three bedroom, two bath house four years after retirement. We were renting a house in town (to faculty) for 20 years, so we were busy with caring for it, also."

Some 45% of our retirees moved, split roughly evenly between those who moved at retirement and those who moved afterwards. Of those who moved, most left the area in which they were living. The three principal reasons for moving (it should be noted that those who moved typically had more than one) are a wish to be closer to family, the desire for a better climate, and an interest in having a more manageable home; a fuller list of reasons is presented in the chart.

REASONS THEY MOVED AT OR AFTER RETIREMENT

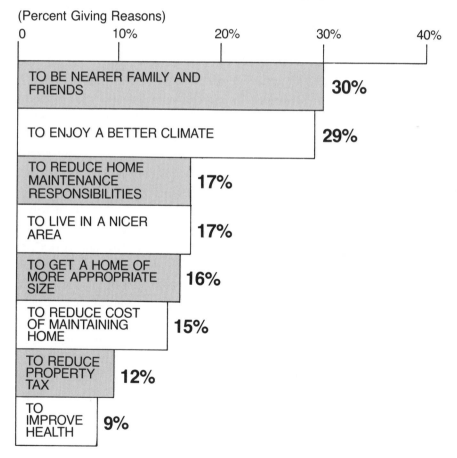

(Percent Giving Reasons)

TO BE NEARER FAMILY AND FRIENDS	**30%**
TO ENJOY A BETTER CLIMATE	**29%**
TO REDUCE HOME MAINTENANCE RESPONSIBILITIES	**17%**
TO LIVE IN A NICER AREA	**17%**
TO GET A HOME OF MORE APPROPRIATE SIZE	**16%**
TO REDUCE COST OF MAINTAINING HOME	**15%**
TO REDUCE PROPERTY TAX	**12%**
TO IMPROVE HEALTH	**9%**

A 79-year-old man says his principal reason for moving was to be near family and friends. He writes: "At retirement, my wife and I moved from a university town in the Midwest to a university town in the South. The move enabled both of us to live near our daughter and her family, and enabled me to collaborate in research with a professor who had earlier been my student in working for his Ph.D. degree. Our daughter and son both have summer homes near the ocean. My research opportunities since retiring have been splendid. In short, family relationships and educational privileges are ideal."

A 64-year-old man and a 67-year-old woman were among those who also moved mainly to be near family and friends. The man writes that "all of our relatives are near enough to join us with only a four hour drive or less" and adds, "You can live where you wish and in our case that meant going to our home in Texas. Gardening can't be beat when you have enough land to plant all you need and more." Says the woman, who is a former hospital worker: "While working I had to live in the city, in a noisy apartment house. Now I live 60 miles from New York in our house surrounded by trees and natural beauty and still I can satisfy my intellectual needs (library, TV, etc.). Arthritis, high blood pressure, and other old age problems do not allow me to work in the garden and walk in the parks as much as I would like to. I think I chose the most rewarding way of retirement by moving close to the family of my son, to my only grandson."

A 69-year-old retired mathematics professor, who cites both a desire for a better climate and health considerations as his primary motivations for moving, writes: "There was one major step that I took upon retirement, namely, I moved to another location, a college town in a nearby state, about 250 miles away. The motivation for this move was to seek a better and healthier climate. Of course this brought up many new problems, but I feel that I made the transition and adjustment satisfactorily. I wonder sometimes if I should have remained in the city where I taught and weathered the fog, rain, and dampness and continued to maintain the associations that I had made over two decades. I've come to the conclusion that what I did was the correct thing and so I have no misgivings and no regrets."

The following 82-year-old man is an example of someone who chose to move for more than one reason — health considerations, a desire to reduce home maintenance duties and property taxes, and to be nearer his summer home. "Deteriorations in the New England city where we had lived with some satisfaction for 30 years were now making it possible for us to seek a change in milieu and intellectual climate," this retiree says. "The places we had lived in since leaving college had shown us that change could be advantageous, and we found that there would be many reasons to seek a new home nearer the summer refuge we had been creating since I had first enjoyed the freedom of tenure, now 35 years. The Nixon advent revived values of investments, the housing shortage brought a good price for a solid New England house, and we returned to Canada to take full advantage of retirement, and escape the Vietnam War. We have a house and an island retreat, 14 miles apart, and I have had two places for study and writing, although one of them is mostly used by my daughter, a Ph.D., who is writing about Canadian economic history. Ten years later, we have no regrets."

Sometimes a move was dictated by family circumstances — to help an elderly parent or other relatives. A 67-year-old man, for example, writes: "My stepson was very ill, a divorce was in process, and a custody fight ended. We came to help him. I want to return to the house we lived in for 26 years and which we still own." For many, the decision to move was part of a longer-term plan. Says a 78-year-old man: "After college and my first teaching days, I knew that I would be returning to the ancestral farm. Here I could write my poems and stories, take pictures, fish, hunt, garden, and play tennis. Ideal to think of and it has worked out that way. I've been here now since 1965." A 65-year-old former building maintenance supervisor moved to a small community and has spent the early years of his retirement building his new home. "The main attraction of retirement," he says, "has been a chance to fulfill a lifelong dream to purchase a small parcel of land (10 acres) in a small farming community, to build my own home, to plant a garden and fruit trees, and to live in peace away from the noise and pollution of the big city."

A 69-year-old woman and her husband retired to the Southwest from the East Coast because they could pursue research interests involving American Indians on site in "an environment that is physically beautiful, socially companionable, professionally stimulating, and that is located within a day's travel of my husband's two sons and grandchildren." A 76-year-old man writes: "I would not do anything differently because I had planned my retirement for years and acquired a place in the country — in the Catskill Mountains — with woods, mountain streams, and plenty of room around me. I also got the necessary equipment and tools to be as self-sufficient as possible."

And a former department chairman, age 67, based his decision to move using this reasoning: "After spending many years in Cleveland, Washington, and Chicago, we like the convenience and security the small city affords, and it has proved to be somewhat cheaper to live here. We deliberately moved to a town we know with relatives and friends — and a state university, from which my wife and I both graduated, that has provided me with an office and library facilities where I spend about 20 hours a week continuing research on a monograph. We are comfortable, except that I feel a bit like Rip Van Winkle coming back after so many years." He adds yet another reason: "I think it a good idea, if one can manage it, to get away from a place where one has been department chairman so that one doesn't seem to be an old overseer coming in to check on the operation."

Some retirees view relocating as an end in and of itself, as an adventure of sorts. Says a 64-year-old man: "I suppose by relocating from the Greater New York area to Georgia, I have missed a great many lifetime friends. But even as a Yankee, I'm quickly making new friends. All this, in my opinion, adds up to one thing: a person *should* retire to an area completely removed and different from that in which he has been living. The challenge of the new offsets the possibility of getting into a rut." Says another 64-year-old man: "Main attractions of retirement: A complete change of lifestyle. Move with your loving wife to a completely new area, with your retirement funds from the sale of your old house, property, and other incomes. Start life anew."

Relocating— Evaluating the Trade-Offs

In discussing the decision about whether to relocate, those who moved report that, although things generally worked out quite well for them, the move sometimes brought unforeseen difficulties. They particularly mention having to give up something of importance. As with many other major decisions in life, trade-offs are involved in a relocation and the retirees stress that this should be kept in mind. A move to sunnier climes, for example, may also mean a move away from cherished friends and relatives. The pleasure of a new home and a new area can be offset somewhat by the many aspects of starting life anew, such as establishing an identity in a new community, becoming comfortable with a new doctor, and finding replacements for favorite stores. A 72-year-old former library director, who moved to the "Mid-South" because of the "better climate, the beautiful scenery, and the lower level of property taxes and living costs" makes the point this way: "I am living where I wish to be— but there is no Shangri-la."

An 80-year-old man recounts the trade-offs he has discovered: "Both wife and self came from same town. We had purchased a wooded tract for retirement — many friends and relatives nearby. Both of us now think this was a mistake. We departed from very close friends and the university and my research. I consider climate important and this was not considered." A 76-year-old man, who has moved to Florida and otherwise enjoys "the richness of cultural endeavors— music, opera, ballet, theater, senior citizen college programs— and weather that permits year-round gardening and that zest to living" also points out that he misses his children, who live in the Northeastern United States and in Guam. "So we do not see them nearly as often as we'd like," he explains. "However, we continue to be amazed at how the telephone helps to shorten the distance, especially from halfway around the world. We live in a very mobile world and separation over long distances is one of the penalties we pay."

On the other hand, a decision to remain in familiar surroundings may be "safe" but one may miss out on pleasing discoveries. The 64-year-old man mentioned earlier in this chapter who moved to Georgia writes: "I am enjoying retirement after 36 years teaching on the university level. I suppose a major part of my contentment is the fact that I moved — almost by sheer luck — from the New York area to the heart of Dixie. In and around New York I could never have been able to afford retirement — but here I live very, very well. For instance, my home (6 rooms, 2 baths, 6 years old) would cost about $120,000 in and around New York. Here I paid a bit over $40,000 and taxes are under $400 per year. This, of course, adds greatly to my contentment. Although I may now lack a bit of the cultural advantages of New York, Atlanta is but a two hour drive away."

These examples illustrate why our retirees urge prospective retirees who are considering relocating to examine as thoroughly as possible the many facets of the housing/location decision. A 65-year-old former engineer, for example, who moved around the time he retired to go to "a better climate" now finds he "misses the change of seasons" and wants to leave. Another retiree, a 68-year-old widow, tells this story and offers this suggestion:

"I approached my new home in Florida rather naively. Because I was very happy with the location I had chosen and the fact that I was building a house with which I am very happy and in a neighborhood I found pleasant, I presupposed that I would also be in tune with my neighbors. But I have since learned that physical factors do not always insure human compatibility. The important message is to investigate any new neighborhood and find out about the opportunities for social and cultural activities, and the chances for continued professional (not necessarily for pay) activities or for choosing a new profession or other form of work. Don't let the glamor of a new move blind you to the reality of the situation. At the present time, I am considering the possibility of moving to another town, not too far from my present location, but with a more cosmopolitan make-up and more cultural activity. But I will first try to evaluate what opportunities might exist for me by making such a move."

A relocation worked out particularly badly for this 76-year-old man. He explains: "We should have checked out Florida for a year, before moving there and setting up a condo apartment, and then finding we were very unhappy away from our children, grandchildren, and lifelong friends. It was a very stressful period to repack and move back to New York, and a very expensive mistake. It was also a mistake to sell our home (after 22 years) and finding the market too expensive after we moved back."

To get the advance knowledge that's needed to make a proper decision, some retirees rely on information from friends or relatives who are already in the area they are considering moving to. "Both my husband and I were big city born and bred but always anxious to get into a country setting," says a 70-year-old. "This we accomplished. Knowing the area in advance in a general way (climate, etc.) is a must when choosing a retirement home. Also it is helpful to have a friend or relative in the vicinity to sort-of break the ice. We've made many new friends, however." Others return to places they've experienced first-hand before. Says a 64-year-old: "My husband and I left a large city and moved to a very small village, one that I grew up in. We did not have to make new friends. We knew when we returned here we could not always conform to the narrow local viewpoint."

Other retirees suggest sampling an area well in advance, perhaps by renting before buying a home. "I don't think there is anything I would have done differently except maybe rent for a year before making a final decision," says a 65-year-old woman. A 91-year-old woman agrees: "If I could go back and start afresh, I would give more consideration to the surrounding area in which the home was situated. I would not be hasty in choosing. I think I'd rent for a period to get the feel of the region and see if it met my needs." A 71-year-old man was particularly thorough in his research, recalling how "three years in advance of my planned retirement, I took a 12-month sabbatical leave which permitted me to do research at two universities of my choice in widely-separated parts of the country that we thought would be desirable places to live in retirement. We are now living happily in one of those areas, and I think we would have been quite happy in the other area also if we had chosen it."

INCIDENTALLY: TIPS ON HOUSING

Our retirees volunteer some practical advice on housing matters — such as taking care of housing arrangements during the pre-retirement or early retirement years when they can be more easily handled.

For example, two septuagenarians suggest that others contemplating retirement repeat what they did. Says a 79-year-old, "We did our best in the years immediately before retirement to get our house and grounds in good shape, especially mechanical equipment such as furnace, plumbing, laundry, and refrigeration equipment." Adds a 73-year-old, "If you buy a home, set up a fund to pay for incidental costs to improve your home, and replace plants and shrubs." And an 85-year-old man writes: "If a couple has several appliances that are fairly old at the time of retirement, they are apt to have large repair or replacement costs. The same could be true if they own an automobile. And if they continue to occupy their old home they must be prepared to meet unexpected repair and replacement bills, some of major proportions."

Being handy around the house can be an asset, retirees also say. "It would have been helpful now if sometime in my life I had learned to be more self-sufficient in such things as auto maintenance and small home repairs," says a 67-year-old woman. Fortunately, she adds, "These are not serious lacks for me because I have kind, well-informed relatives." Her point is echoed by a 76-year-old man, who says, "Very early in my life I would have learned to become proficient in the use of hand tools and learned about the hundred and one items that one meets up with in owning his own home."

As far as choosing a new home is concerned, several retirees note that one should keep in mind that personal energy levels may decline with age. "I would prefer less house to care for," writes a 68-year-old woman. A 70-year-old man would have "rearranged my living arrangements to reduce housekeeping and property management requirements *sooner*. This should be done early in retirement when one has the physical strength and mental capacity for the necessary decisions and labor." And a 79-year-old man says simply: "Get a one-story, not a two-story, house."

Among the things to look for in making the relocation decision, continues the 91-year-old woman mentioned above, is the intellectual environment. "I think I'd look into the possibility of a college town," she says, "because of the opportunity it offers for mental stimulation and recreation." Another older retiree, an 85-year-old man, agrees. "Perhaps we should mention that we live in a college town," he says. "We constantly come in contact with the student body, which perhaps gives us a more youthful outlook on life."

Indeed, some retirees, such as the following 74-year-old man, view intellectual harmony as the most critical factor to consider. "I retired to a place that is almost ideal with respect to climate and opportunities for outdoor recreation," he writes. "Its principal lack is in people with similar intellectual and cultural interests to my own. At the time for retirement I might have found a place that offered both a warm climate and kindred spirits, but there seems to be a scarcity of such places." A mix of age groups is the key to a stimulating environment, according to the following 73-year-old. He writes: "We stayed in our own community for several years before moving down with the cotton heads of the south. Probably we'd have done better had we stayed in a more normal mix of old and young. We have many new friends, yet wish there were even more young people in the street."

Another factor to consider in making the move-or-stay decision is the importance of physical proximity to family and friends. For example, a 74-year-old man who says that in his retirement home he "enjoys being away from the cold North, being outside most of year — I swim daily in the pool — and participating in the condominium's Board of Directors," adds that, "instead of moving to a Florida condo from the New York area, which was attractive at the time because of the better climate, I would more carefully look into being away so far from family." And a 73-year-old woman who relocated says, "I think I would consider living in the same area, although I didn't like the climate, because that's where long-time friends are," while a 67-year-old woman says simply, "I would not have moved to another area so far from the children."

In addition to the people-part of the retirement location decision, our retirees say that the quality of retirement life can be further enhanced by easy access to a library and other cultural facilities, nearness to medical facilities and retail stores, and the efficiency of the local transportation system — and this suggests yet more factors to check out in making the decision whether or not to move.

The 91-year-old woman writes: "I'd be more thoughtful about looking into the services of the neighborhood — the daily living needs, such as food, drugs, clothing, hospital, doctor, dentist, and other essential health services. Since weather has more effect on the elderly, though not much attention is given to the topic, I'd look more seriously into the overall record of the climate. All the above is hindsight after having come from an old settled neighborhood to a comparatively young development." Says a 70-year-old woman, "Moving into a rural area, I did, and do, miss the shopping advantages of a larger community and the cultural activities, and my husband has found that it is difficult to obtain materials for his hobbies." According to a 65-year-old man: "My only drawback is being 25 miles from the closest medical services available to us. Also, for decent prices, we have to travel 100 miles to do our marketing, possibly once a month. I would have bought land closer to the big city (within 50 miles)."

In discussing the availability of basic services, a 68-year-old woman recalls: "I was not prepared for the difficulties of finding our way around towns surrounding us, change of stores where we shopped and finding articles we needed (such as our favorite brand of shoes), selection of new doctors, dentists, and hospitals, learning names and facts about so many new acquaintances all at once. I am not sure that I would again decide to move to another area." Her uneasiness was aggravated by a series of health problems. She recalls: "The choice of the best surgeon and hospital on short notice was difficult in an area I was unfamiliar with. Although I was lucky enough to choose an excellent surgeon and hospital, I might have felt a little easier to have been in our old home, where I was more familiar with the doctors and hospitals."

A 69-year-old man says he misses "the abundant library facilities to which I was accustomed. I would — other things being equal — locate in an area where library facilities, both general and specialized, are abundant and readily accessible." In contrast, a 73-year-old points out that "the library facilities are good because of inter-library loans. We also maintain library contacts in the metropolitan area." He adds: "Because we are located in rural Missouri we do not see friends and acquaintances as often as we might wish. The distance factor, combined with higher gasoline prices, restricts or limits maintaining contacts with members of the department and attending interesting seminars."

Some retirees who relocated write that they miss their former institutions and the roles they played at them. "If I could," says a 68-year-old man, "I would choose the institution to retire from in the vicinity of my stay. The changing of place, in my case, cuts you off from university life and deprives the retiree from many benefits and privileges you could enjoy otherwise." Another 68-year-old man writes: "We moved 350 miles from our family and friends and home for 36 years. I miss the power base for assisting my students and friends in achieving their academic and personal goals. At first it was a little difficult to adjust to a conservative rural farming community having come from a liberal, urbanized, industrialized city. It is good, though, to be free from tight schedules and countless committee meetings, and to have leisure time to pursue personal interests and hobbies."

A 64-year-old recounts his feelings at some length. Even though he left friends of over 20 years, he writes that he is happy with his move "to a pleasant village close to a culturally interesting and pleasing small city and equally close to several small colleges, proximity to family (both mine and my wife's), and our ready acceptance in our new community, where we find new friends and new opportunities for community service and activities." However, he continues, "I miss the institutional structure, including the routines which were at the center of my professional life for 30 years, with its built-in supports and familiar ways. Being a part-time participant in another institution near here is not the same; though I hope that my relationship with this institution will be of long standing and provide me with these 'supports,' etc., for another five or six years at least."

The following retiree, age 71, describes how he and his wife are trying to take advantage of the best of both worlds. He writes: "Our lifestyle is somewhat simpler than when we lived in a 14-room house, but we enjoy our new condominium on the ocean which is furnished with our cherished antiques. We have kept a small apartment in the city where I taught so that I can still have some contact with the university and so that we can maintain the social contacts which mean so much to us."

The retirees point out that they've met new friends, sometimes very easily, though sometimes after a period of adjusting to their new locale. "There is a disadvantage of moving to a new community. But I thoroughly recommend a total change of living although it takes a little time to become involved," says a 65-year-old woman. Adds a 65-year-old man: "We've left behind the cold and gloom of the Midwest and live in an almost perfect dry and sunny climate. One misses old friends, of course, but moving away was a free choice which, all things considered, I do not regret. One can make friends in any inhabited place. And we still have mail and phone service!"

When all the factors in the housing/relocation decision are weighed, a final judgment ultimately depends on individual tastes. That point shows up most strikingly in the paired *Essays*, "Two Views of a Big City," which describe the very different feelings of two of our retirees living in the same metropolis.

ESSAYS: TWO VIEWS OF A BIG CITY

"all our New York City friends forecast disaster"

I cannot imagine any decision more rewarding than the one we made — being able to live in a small village rather than in New York City!

We own our home and live where it is quiet, and beautiful, and where people care for each other. Living in a small town, in the beautiful mountains of upstate New York, is an entirely new experience and one both my husband and I enjoy to the fullest. And owning an automobile, which provides a sense of freedom hard to describe. There is no public transportation whatsoever in our county. Cannot imagine a better choice than the one we made.

All our New York City friends forecast disaster. All have visited and expressed envy (whether out of politeness we will never know, nor do we care — we like it). Believe it or not, we have found no drawbacks! It may be a different story if we last to our upper 80s and early 90s, but I doubt it. As realistically, we don't expect miracles, but we expect to be able to cope — unless senility be our lot!

We have taken to country living (gardening, hiking, community service, plenty of reading, music). Plus a cat, who thinks she is a person, and a dog, who is sure he is a person. We were both city people, and the 13 years since retirement have been a totally different and utterly satisfying life.

I personally must confess to being somewhat nervous about it all, for it at times seems too good, too lucky, to be true. But to date it is.

— 75-year-old married woman

"my enjoyment comes from opportunities . . . unique to New York City"

I'm having a marvelous time.

Every year during my working years, when I read the Metropolitan Museum's lecture series, there was always at least one I would have loved to go to — but they were always during the day. Now I can go not only to lecture series, but I also drop in to the Museum (I live within walking distance) once every week or two. And I'm thoroughly enjoying courses in classics at a New York City college, which has a senior citizens' program under which one pays no tuition, only a $25 registration fee. And I can do all this and get up at 8:30, instead of 7:00 as when I was working.

What planning I did for retirement has turned out, so far, not to be relevant. I had concluded that, as a single woman with no living relatives, the appropriate arrangement for me was a life-care community. Several years before I retired I began collecting information about such communities, and visited two or three. And my increasing involvement in an outreach program for elderly people is leading me to reconsider whether a life-care community is necessarily the best arrangement. At the very least, I am deferring that for as long as I continue to enjoy my present situation.

I also thought I'd like to live someplace where one could sit outdoors comfortably for more of the year than is possible in New York. However, in the almost two years that I've been retired, I'm finding that much of my enjoyment comes from opportunities that, if not unique to New York City, are certainly more plentiful and more easily accessible here.

—68-year-old single woman

Retirement Communities And Retirement Homes

As is true of retired people in general, a small proportion of our retirees live in retirement communities. A 79-year-old widow describes how she made her decision not to enter a retirement community. She writes: "My retirement is satisfying as of now. But what of the years ahead? Should I have paid in to a retirement community that gives full care? Many of my associates have — and have urged it on me. I consider my health history and the statistics, and I have elected to live out my life in my own home and look forward to a brief terminal illness when the time comes." And a 74-year-old woman, who has lived in the same house for 30 years, points out that "neither my husband or I like the idea of retirement homes where all are senior citizens, segregated from younger people."

Some retirees did choose to move to retirement communities, where they may own a house, condominium, or apartment and be around people of similar age; some of these communities may offer limited medical care as well. Retirement communities attract retirees of all ages. A 65-year-old married man, for example, has embraced his retirement community particularly enthusiastically. In retirement, he writes, "I can unleash some creativity which has been bottled up inside me for years," adding, in describing his favorite activities, "I write, tell, and sing comedy jokes and folk songs for my age group." Among the other attractions, he continues, are that, "I can start a preventive health program so that I can enjoy my retirement years feeling good physically; live in the Sunshine State (I always feel better about myself and my neighbors when the sun is shining); and live with others sharing these same priorities in this beautiful retirement community." And a 71-year-old married man writes: "This large retirement community of about 22,000 persons— average age is 72 or 73— provides a tremendous variety of facilities, activities, and organizations that enable interested people to keep active. It also provides security and services that nowadays are reassuring and also make travel more convenient. On the other hand, one is all too frequently reminded of one's mortality by the death of an acquaintance or a friend. But it is also pleasant to see 80 or 90-year-olds who are physically active, mentally alert, and involved in all sorts of programs. A frequently heard comment is, 'I'm busier now than before I retired.'"

Retirees in older age groups, however, were more prone than younger ones to write about their retirement communities. Among them was an 84-year-old unmarried woman, who notes how "ownership in real estate (a duplex) gave me the investment security to buy into an unusually comfortable and unique retirement community. There is plenty of companionship, and opportunity for self-expression and independence." An 82-year-old married man says that, "We live in a splendid retirement community and the main attractions are security, pleasant surroundings and congenial friends, and freedom from nagging responsibilities."

An 81-year-old man comments that "a state of health enjoyed by my wife and me that has made our retirement years a source of continuing alertness, both mental and physical, and provided a sense of well-being and happiness. For our remaining years we now live in a retirement community with full health care facilities and other services provided especially for care of aging people. Our son and family live within convenient driving distance." An 85-year-old woman, who is divorced, adds: "The disadvantages are less due to retirement than to sheer old age. I just ran down and my old friends gradually died off. I found myself being a bit stranded. Here in this retirement complex I find interesting people — people who can share my past and my memories."

Our retirees also discuss life-care communities, a special kind of living arrangement that includes lifelong medical and nursing care. An 83-year-old married man writes: "My retirement was fortunate and uneventful until 1980 due to having a house and sufficient income — annuities, dividends — to manage without worry. When my eyes went we had already signed up for a comfortable retirement home, with 'living care.' We entered in 1980 and have a comfortable apartment. The sale of our house provided for capital that gives us about 30% of our income.

I feel that we have been lucky!" To a 75-year-old single woman, "The life-care community in which I am living is a very good answer to retirement problems. I live in an apartment with my sister. We have housekeeping care. We may eat one, two, or three meals a day in the main dining room. (We *must* eat one meal there.) We have health care to the end of our days, in a medical center here or in a hospital. There are all kinds of activities in which we may engage."

ESSAY: "LIFE IS WHAT YOU MAKE IT"

Life is what you make it. It is a beautiful world and there are wonderful people in it. I was left an orphan at 14 years, was clothed and fed by my mother's family as one of theirs'. A short marriage not a success, but I had a profession (nursing). I could work any where in the world, which I did in China, and on the way home, Rome. Travel was my greatest interest. The great outdoors always around me.

In December 1969 I bought into a retirement home in a nice area in California — an area that has been my home base since 1902 — for security in declining years. We have a licensed long-term nursing hospital. The residents are mostly professional people, retired after successful business lives. I never expected to live to my present age, as I have outlived all relatives of my era. If I outlive my finances, the retirement home will never put me out. I am lucky to be here.

Retirement is worth working towards. If possible, retire early enough to enjoy its possibilities. So much of interest to be had without great wealth. So far have had 22 years of it, met wonderful people, learned much, and enjoyed unexpected friendships.

—92-year-old divorced woman

A number of our older retirees reside in retirement homes, which often consist of cooperative living arrangements that provide nursing care. The following married woman, age 82, offers these pros and cons of retirement homes. She observes: "At ages 58 and 60 we retired, left the city, moved to a small retirement home in an attractive town of 6,000. Here we are relieved of all yard work and house work. We are served three meals a day, have maid service every 2 weeks, and there is a nurse on duty. We can be as active as we wish and socialize as much or as little as we wish. In all, it's a lifestyle that suits us although there are disadvantages. The living quarters in these retirement homes are too small. There's too much togetherness. There are always transportation problems. It is difficult to make new friends in retirement years."

An 87-year-old single woman remains on her own for now but believes a retirement home is inevitable. She writes: "I found it very profitable to share with friends in buying a house before retirement and sharing equally in the expenses of home maintenance and living expenses. If I was not so situated I would find it difficult to have adequate living conditions under my present income. I have also entered my name in a church retirement home and I believe this is imperative planning for every person over 75 years of age and earlier, depending on the physical condition. I believe one should remain independent as long as feasibly possible but one should be willing to accept living in a more protected environment when that seems necessary. This is especially true at present when it is very expensive to have 24-hour care in the home." An 89-year-old widow, currently in a retirement home, echoes her comments about a retirement home's advantages, stating, "I like the security I get from living in a retirement home: to know I'll be taken care of when sick, that I'll never have to move again, and that I have friends around me for company when I want it. I do not have to get out in bad weather for anything."

Chapter 11: RELATIONSHIPS

Friendships

The preceding chapters mainly cover our retirees' thoughts about changes they experienced in adjusting to their new retirement lifestyle. Intertwined with these experiences were other changes — modifications, shifts, and, sometimes, breaks— in their relationships with former colleagues, students, friends, and even with spouses.

Colleagues. A 61-year-old woman, who retired relatively young at the time her older husband did, notes how "a drawback of retirement is having to make new friends because most of your friends are in the academic field and are still working." While it might be expected that comparatively young retirees would miss their peers, the feeling of loss of peer comradeship was also keenly expressed by many older retirees. "The main drawback is that one loses touch with one's former colleagues and suddenly you are on the shelf," writes a 71-year-old woman. "You're automatically thought of as 'older.' It is a more difficult task to maintain friendships with the younger people one formerly saw much of."

A 74-year-old man says that, while his former university colleagues' "intentions are good, when you retire you scarcely hear from them, except when fund-raising events are taking place. Remember the old adage: out of sight, out of mind." Writes an 86-year-old widow: "For a highly trained *professional* actively engaged in group work, the cut-off from fellow workers, still in the midst of things, can be devastating. Membership in the professional and honor societies seems hollow." Adds a 72-year-old man, "The only drawback to retirement I can think of is you are not associating with the people you worked with and you lose a lot of friends by not associating with them."

An 80-year-old former medical school department chairman misses his former colleagues, but he's put his feelings into perspective. He writes: "I was involved with the young house officers and Ph.D.s in the laboratory. I also miss the daily contacts with my professional colleagues, and the administrators of the hospital. Most of all, I think, I miss my daily contacts with young doctors. When you have retired you become very much aware of the fact that you no longer contribute very much to your old department and have no right to expect it will continue to operate as you may think it should. You are very much in the position of a father after the children are gone and begin to run their own lives. This can be depressing unless you admit to yourself that it is as it should be."

Of course, some retirees welcome the change from the job — and don't mind missing former colleagues. A 69-year-old man, for example, expresses "relief from the contentious aspects of the job" — a point made on previous pages by retirees who are relieved that they no longer face such things as the pressures of peer competition, disagreement with a superior's policies, and the boredom of committee meetings. Adds a 77-year-old man: "The obvious main attraction in favor of retirement at a reasonable age — between 65 and 70 — lies in the relaxing experience which comes from relief from the pressures of academic life and its routines. All other attractions are subordinate thereto."

Students. Some retired educators fondly recall their students and the interplay between teacher and pupil. "The only drawback to retirement has been the loss of contact with young people of college age and with college scholars. I miss both the mental stimulus and the social contacts that my work provided," says a 69-year-old woman. "In my case," writes a 72-year-old widow, "the main drawback is the absence of daily contact with young people of college age. I never met a bore among them. Some of them can on occasion irk or annoy you, but they never bore you." A 72-year-old man misses "very much the close contact of working and advising young men." Adds a 61-year-old woman: "I miss being around the students. They keep you young."

However, a 61-year-old man writes: "Occasionally I miss the regular contact with teenagers, but that is more than offset by having the time to maintain better correspondence with old friends. Living in the same community where I worked, I am able to see or talk with my former colleagues regularly; I would miss them if I had to live elsewhere. I certainly do not miss grading papers or teaching the same old lessons year after year."

Friends, old and new. Relationships with friends can also be affected by retirement. For example, relocations at or during retirement can affect the retirees who stay behind as well as those who move. A 67-year-old-man is in the first category, and he writes: "Many of our peers left for other retirement areas and this leaves a void in socialization unless one follows." A 65-year-old man in the second category — who says "we came to this area only about 10 years ago, and most of our friends, the friends of our youth and early middle age, live at a distance from us" — muses at length on some of the difficulties he's encountered in making friends in his new area:

"The drawbacks of retirement seem mainly to be related to friendships and contacts with compatible people. Friendships seem to be related to age brackets and, at the age of my wife and myself, most contemporaries have already firmly established a circle of friends and are not interested in expending the effort required to include new people among those already in the circle. The friendship problem is still a mystery. How we could have better prepared ourselves in this area is not at all clear. I believe that friendships are built upon, among other things, shared experiences and that if you move later in life away from old haunts and friends, it becomes difficult to make new friends, both for the reasons cited above and also because you have less time and opportunity to have shared experiences with people your own age."

As we have seen in earlier chapters, some of these difficulties are related to the loss of an institutional setting that one has become used to over many years. For example, a 72-year-old man says there may be a problem of mental wavelength. "The trouble with university or academic employment is that retirees from other lines of work seem rather uninteresting persons," he writes. "Snobbery? I don't think so — just a factual difference in mental activity. I have been used to considering ideas — good and bad — but other retirees have not. Consequently, I get most of my mental stimulation from books and journals." In a similar vein, a 68-year-old woman writes: "Persons with whom we now associate are mostly retired military or businessmen and their academic background is not commensurate with ours. Hence, our contacts are pleasant but seldom stimulating."

Here's how a former career woman, now 72 and a widow, describes the mental wavelength problem: "Though I mix easily with people socially, I have found it difficult to find someone intellectually compatible among the women my age living in this condominium complex. Most are widows who spent their lives keeping house and raising families. I spent my life pursuing a career and doing many interesting things. As a result we have little in common. I don't enjoy listening to others' tales of 'when John was alive,' and their constant talk of children and grand-children, *ad infinitum*. The age group I enjoy most are 'young folks' in their late 40s and early 50s. They are still out in the world doing things— and I can identify with this."

A frustrated 82-year-old woman offers a different view of the attitudes of middle-aged people. She complains: "The elderly are categorized. Thus: townspeople treat me as a person until they learn that I have a cottage in a retirement home. At once I become, not an individual, but a sweet little old lady who is not quite bright. Many old people consider themselves ancient and helpless, but we are as different one from another as we were before reaching 65. It is usually the middle-aged who discrimi-nate, perhaps because they feel threatened. The young are much more likely to treat one as a person."

Events not related to retirement, such as the loss of a spouse through death or divorce, can also hamper a retiree's ability to maintain friendships. A 70-year-old divorced woman describes the predicament a newly single person faces in a circle of friends who are couples: "In spite of a great deal of club and other social activities, I am alone too much. Don't know how to correct this, as almost all of my friends are still married— therefore not free for bridge, movies, etc. in evenings and over weekends." And of course advancing age itself takes its toll. "The worst drawback of being retired and old is that almost all the friends I had are now dead," says an 82-year-old woman. Observes a 70-

year-old man, "After retirement, one's circle of intimate friends decreases, even though the number of acquaintances increases."

Nevertheless, our retirees report that new friends can be made — sometimes easily, and sometimes it has to be worked at. Says a 73-year-old man: "You surely have to put forth that extra effort and that is not easy to do. Inviting people to your home is always extra work, but you must set the example or people will pass you by." Some retirees suggest making that "extra effort" during the working years by not letting daily job concerns overwhelm one's social relationships. Says a 74-year-old psychologist, "I would have spent less time in my area of specialization and more time in making and keeping friends." A 71-year-old woman agrees: "I should have depended less on my working colleagues and developed closer friends outside my employment field." A 75-year-old woman believes she should have made her "extra effort" to make new friends during the early years of her retirement. "I should have joined more groups," she says. "I never bothered in the early years — too much to keep me active and interested otherwise. Group activity can be a bore, but *does* maintain contact with people into the late and inactive years, or years of failing health."

Undeniably, for many people retirement can be a time of enhanced friendships. A 74-year-old widow describes "more frequent contacts with friends, old and new, some of whom are now also retired and free to plan activities together." Another widow, age 67, points out she's "making new friends and enjoying the old, at a much more leisurely pace." A married man, age 69, comments: "It is especially nice to do things on the spur of the moment with our close friends, such as eating out, taking a trip, or just socializing." And a 71-year-old man, who's single, says: "Developing a new lifestyle was a challenge. I enjoyed exploring a new and different community and finding a place in it." And that includes, he adds, "meeting many people, some of whom have become friends." Adds an unmarried woman, also 71: "A drawback to retirement is the breaking of close ties with the business or educational facilities one has enjoyed being involved with for so long. However, new friends are made and there is more time to spend with long-time friends."

Husbands and Wives

Almost 90% of the men who responded to our survey, and one-third of the women, are married. According to their comments, retirement may cause married retirees to reach new accommodations with their spouses — the equivalent, perhaps, of a honeymoon agreement on how to squeeze the toothpaste tube. A 70-year-old woman notes, for example, that "a main drawback of retirement is having one's husband constantly underfoot." A 75-year-old man says simply, "Some couples find that there is too much 'togetherness' after retiring and they get bickering over little decisions." A 72-year-old man elaborates: "Adjustments are needed in home and domestic affairs. This element is more than both husband and wife at home all or much of the time involving extra meal preparation. Decisions on minor matters, such as the temperature of the house, which were for many years made by wife or husband now become an area of disagreement. In a way, retirement requires a redefinition of the husband/wife roles and respective responsibilities." Many husbands and wives have successfully developed new arrangements. A 77-year-old husband, for example, explains, "Fortunately my wife and I have many activities we both enjoy, and both share equally with household chores (cleaning, bedmaking, dishwashing, shopping). I don't attempt to do much cooking. At that I'm not much good."

A 69-year-old man notes the potential problem and a possible solution. In retirement, he observes, "The time now becomes available to enter into a more intimate and deeper relationship with spouse, children, grandchildren, and friends. This aspect of retirement is hazardous if not approached with caution and thoughtfulness. If one is living with spouse (or other person) the increase in amount of time the two spend together may emphasize, if not exaggerate, what each considers a fault in the other. To avoid this problem it is essential, at least, that the spouse of the retired person should have been in *full* agreement about the idea of retirement."

ESSAY: "ONE MORE CHILD TUGGING AT HER SKIRT!"

As a woman, my life has been governed, more or less, by "interruptions" — unexpected demands on my time and strength. Now, my husband is learning more about what that means. He is learning to do more around the house; I am learning to let him do more.

When we were first married, we were in graduate school and shared housework. Soon after, when I was earning my PHT — Putting Hubby Through — we did even more such sharing, and this continued after World War II, when we were both teaching in college full-time and had two small children. But we then had two more children, and I stopped teaching and spent 15 years being a full-time housewife and at least a half-time volunteer before I returned to teaching to help our children through college. My husband left teaching (to replace two teaching salaries) but eventually returned to academia in an administrative role. Thus he got out of the habit of helping at home, and I forgot how helpful he had been.

This was an adjustment difficult for us both for about six months. A little more thought and planning could have made the transition easier. Ideally, I applaud constant sharing, but it isn't always possible. Awareness of the need for such sharing (and frictions involved) could be taught in a pre-retirement course. Such instruction and pre-retirement discussion could eliminate: "I don't know where anything is kept!" "Just show me how!" "Why won't you let me do anything?" "I'd just like to help." "What can I do next?" To a woman (used to doing everything for herself), these questions and statements make her feel that she suddenly has one more child tugging at her skirt! Such instruction could also eliminate the husband's sudden "takeover" and directions about what and when and how to do things that the wife has been doing as a matter of course for years.

—65-year-old woman

Beginning the retirement years in tandem was a related proposal (although that strategy poses difficulties if a younger spouse is actively pursuing a career). "The only thing I would have liked to have done differently," says a 66-year-old man, "is to have encouraged my wife to retire at the same time. The five or six years of age difference between men and women— at least in my case — can bring about a problem that must be handled quite diplomatically and with great sensitivity. When both are working and sharing household chores, fine. But if one retires and the other does not, the possible danger the retiree may find is that he (or she) has given up a good post in order to become a 100% household drudge. However, the younger individual may not wish to retire. Well, you see the problem. Fortunately we seem never to have let it become the problem that others have." Similarly, a 64-year-old wife notes, "It is a drawback if both spouses do not retire at the same time. My husband retired five years before I did and I held him back from doing many things that we were looking forward to. Before I could retire, he became ill and this has cut back many of our plans."

One husband, who is 64, hopes that semi-retirement will help him and his wife adjust. "My wife and I are having to learn that retirement involves unexpected adjustments," he writes. "She reminds me that she has *not* retired as a (conscientious — my view) homemaker. We are having to work out personal schedules and the allotment of responsibilities in the light of my new status. Since I shall be shortly doing part-time teaching, these problems may be better solved." Says a 69-year-old: "With my wife still working and not real well, I do a lot of the housework and some of the food preparation. Having the office to go to about four days a week — I sell real estate — saves me from being a full-time house-husband. Perhaps the work activity saves me from another type drawback, namely, a feeling of being out of things." Cautions a 65-year-old man, "It is important to make commitments of your time with your spouse and without your spouse. She too has a retirement adjustment of importance to face." As a 66-year-old wife says: "This matter of a partner with whom one can share the pleasures of retirement is not always within the scope of one's choosing. (If a spouse is not available, a good friend might be.) Even if the sharing consists only of having someone to tell about the newest activity, or the newest ideas, it would seem to have immeasurable value. You do not have to live in each other's pockets. Of all our classes — I've started a number of very interesting art and art-related courses after a career in math and science — my husband and I share only one. We therefore have so much to tell each other when we get together at dinner time."

Once the necessary adjustments to retirement are made, our retirees write how retirement also offers an opportunity for many husbands and wives to discover each other anew. Some wives write that they welcome the increased presence of their husbands. "Not until my husband also retired," says a 61-year-old wife, "did I really *have* a husband." Adds a 64-year-old wife: "Having a husband, who formerly traveled, at home most of the time is *so* wonderful. We enjoy doing things together as well as doing some of our own things." Similar sentiments were expressed by husbands. A 67-year-old man, for example, notes "the availability of time to enjoy the company of my wife, rather than both being too busy to companion one another."

Both husbands and wives pointed out how retirement added new dimensions to their relationships. Writes an 81-year-old, "I am enjoying immensely the fact that my wife and I are growing closer and closer." A 66-year-old wife has this to say: "Part of my pleasure in my retirement lies in sharing it with my husband, who retired two years before I did. His activities rather paved the way for me. We both belong to an organization of retired professionals which presents classes for its membership and is taught by members. It is an important part of our activities; we each take three classes. He also built a darkroom at home a couple of years before he retired, and gradually increased the time he spends there. His joy in retirement set the stage for me. As I tell my former colleagues, it is important to retire *to* — not *from*."

Indeed, marriage can be a most treasured resource in retirement. Says a 71-year-old wife, "I have always enjoyed being married. My first husband died. My present one is the nicest person I've ever known. We enjoy each other." As shown in the *Comments* section below, many husbands similarly describe happy relationships with their wives in retirement.

COMMENTS: "WE HAPPEN TO LOVE EACH OTHER"

The real secret of my retirement is an excellent wife, who is her own self-starter, and a congenial but clear-cut acceptance between us of our separate responsibilities and expectations, each from the other. Not incidentally, we happen to love each other.

—67-year-old husband

The presence of a fine wife who is a real comrade, and our deep commitment to the Quaker faith, has done so much to give us strength for the stretch of our lives.

—81-year-old husband

I am married to the finest person that ever lived.

—78-year-old husband

My wife and I were school kids together in the fourth grade. After marriage at 25 and 26 years of age, we raised four children. One of the things I enjoy in retirement is being together with this gal 24 hours of each day. I think she feels the same.

—70-year-old husband

My wife suggests that I might be happier in my retirement with a younger and more energetic wife; I doubt it.

—75-year-old husband

We have been happily married for 58 years and still retain our sense of humor . . .

—85-year-old husband

Marriage and Divorce in Later Life

Some retirees were married late in life. They include a 75-year-old woman who retired, following administrative work in the agricultural field in the Mideast, in order to marry at the age of 58, and a 69-year-old woman who retired at age 59 to both marry for the first time and care for aged parents.

"We are enjoying our retirement," the 69-year-old writes. "My husband likes to work in the yard and I like to work indoors, and we have many interests outside our home. I can practice my music. Church activities have always had high priority in our lives. We travel some and enjoy seeing new places. I guess I must say we are quite contented and retirement has been a pleasant experience for both of us." A 75-year-old former hospital worker, who married a year after she retired at age 65, is also happy in her late-life marriage. She comments: "I like a home, and to have someone to share it with undoubtedly has made my retirement years so good, especially when my spouse is such a nice person and we are so compatible."

One retiree, a 66-year-old divorced man, wonders whether he should remarry. "If my ex-wife would have fitted my ideal better and I would have fitted hers better," he writes, "then retirement would be more satisfying. This makes me feel disloyal to my present friend, but I can't seem to dispel my doubts about whether we should 'cement' our relationship and get married."

Only about 5% of the retirees were separated or divorced at the time of our survey. A few couples faced separation or divorce in their early retirement years, perhaps because the natural tensions of getting used to a new lifestyle in retirement caused deeper-rooted problems to surface. Retirement-related tensions may have been a factor in the separation of a 65-year-old man from his much younger wife. In explaining his view of what led to his pending divorce, this man writes: "My wife did not care for wintering in Florida at all— surrounded by so many 70, 80 and 90-year-olds. And as my physical activity decreased due to a coronary, hers increased— more tennis than ever, even jogging. Differences became magnified and after a seemingly minor spat, she left." He adds: "The attractions of retirement are many, if one has a helpmate to share them with. If not, then get one."

A 66-year-old's divorce seems to have had a happier ending. He writes: "My own retirement was followed by five years of very active participation in my wife's business. For reasons unfathomable, she decided, at age 64, that she wanted a divorce. So after a period of readjustment, I found another partner. We are exceptionally compatible and, with approximately equal incomes, are living a very good life, and look forward to many years of happy companionship."

Family

Some retirees mention their relationships with children, parents, siblings, and other relatives. Like so many of the responses on other subjects, these run the gamut.

Several portray a rich network of ties within very extended families. A 72-year-old, widowed at the age of 24, names "time to be with my family" as the first advantage of retirement. "Yes, I live alone," she writes, "but now I can travel to see members of my family, especially my son, his wife, and my two grandchildren, and to spend my summers at camp in Vermont where I am joined by nieces, nephews, sisters-in-law, brothers-in-law, and members of my husband's family." A 74-year-old married man marvels at his good fortune, stating: "Retirement is more rewarding than I expected; also more than I deserve. Half of that is good luck; the other half is the only partly earned good relations with an extended family and with a number of friends, far and near. I see no way I could have influenced that luck or those relations." And a 65-year-old unmarried woman cites as one of retirement's attractions "living among relatives whom I haven't seen for years."

As you might expect, retirees often derive great emotional gratification from their children and their children's children. "We have two wonderful and devoted children, one an M.D. and the other a J.D.," exclaims an 81-year-old man, who also reports how happy he is with his 52-year-old marriage. A newly-retired man, age 65, is happy about "the ability to visit our children, who are spread out from coast to coast, and to become acquainted with our grandchildren as they grow up," just as a 72-year-old man welcomes the "time to enjoy grandchildren, our children, and their friends." Another retiree, age 71, recounts how he and his wife "enjoy working and having fun with our kids who are 16 and 14 years old. I realize that my situation is unusual since I am surrounded by young people who do their best to keep me young, too."

ESSAY: "WE ARE NOT DEPENDENT UPON CLOSE FAMILY TIES . . ."

My wife and I have had no children. Thus, although I am sure we have missed a lot of enrichment that children would have brought to our lives, we have avoided a common mistake that many retirees have made, with their lives having become too closely tied to their children and grandchildren. We have made lives for ourselves and we are not dependent upon close family ties, although we keep in touch with our relatives. In time, of course, we may regret not having closer family ties. But I don't think so.

Just as we looked ahead to retirement and made plans well in advance, we expect in time to move into a life-care residence when we become less able to care for ourselves, and here we expect to enjoy the fellowship of other persons similarly-situated. We have the financial means to make this kind of arrangement; we are not on "easy street" financially, but we are comfortable and reasonably secure. My wife was employed also for a number of years, and she has a modest retirement income from that employment. And we have no children to support and put through college.

Think about retirement a long time in advance. Don't become so completely wrapped up in your job that there is nothing left of yourself when you are no longer employed. With broad interests and wide participation in enjoyable activities, retirement provides new opportunities — the chance to read all the books you never had time for before, and the chance to do all the interesting things you never had time for before. And don't become so fully attached to family and old friends that you cannot make a new life for yourself apart from them. Rewarding friendships can be established anywhere, if you enter into the life of the community. We have lived in many different places across the years, and we have been reasonably happy every place we have lived.

— 71-year-old married man

In a similar vein, a 66-year-old woman embraces retirement as an "opportunity for development of more meaningful relationships with adults and children. This factor grows in importance with each passing day." An 85-year-old man dwells on the subject at some length: "We are fortunate to have two families of grandchildren who do not live far from us, and we get to see them quite often. We enjoy them very much and it has been a great pleasure to watch them grow from tiny babies to married adults, and to learn from them what the young people are thinking these days. Through the years we have tried diligently not to spoil them and I believe we have succeeded, as one of our granddaughters told a friend of hers that we (her grandparents), are 'cool.' Our grandchildren are nearly grown up now, but during the past year we have begun interest in another generation, as we now have two great-grandchildren."

A former professor is delighted to be "free to educate my three grandchildren." A woman who seems to have found widowhood particularly traumatic takes solace in "a very loving son. So by and large, I have no complaints." Another retiree— who says "I hope that I have not become maudlin" in doing so — writes the following: "The family becomes a valuable asset in the future (today's present). We have been married and true to each other for over 45 years now. We have 4 children, 19 grandchildren. Our early sacrifices and concern for the children are now paying off. They have matured well, we all get together often, we help each other when in trouble, and we enjoy each other's company. It is not that I would have done differently with family. It is just that it seems now to be important — terribly important — that we did encourage these assets as we matured and so today it is all paying off."

However, "how to get along with children" is specifically mentioned as a difficulty in retirement by at least one retiree, and is hinted at by others, although no one chose to write in detail about the matter. Some people who experienced troubles with children often experienced troubles with parents also, like the 63-year-old who warns others cryptically against "parents' or children's misfortunes requiring physical and/or financial assistance." A 66-year-old likewise cautions, "Grown up children do experience financial and health problems and aged parents need care and attention." As a result, he continues, "Planning for retirement should not be focused on the individual's needs and goals alone but also include the possibility of continuing family responsibilities." Indeed, one man, age 71, worries: "One big, big drawback in my idyllic world is the future of my adult son, unemployed and dependent upon me." And a 73-year-old man grumbles, "When I retired I did not expect to acquire a wife and two children, or be faced with $12,000 a year tuition bills for New York private schools."

Caring for Relatives

In these days of ever-increasing life spans, many younger retirees find themselves providing live-in care to ailing parents or siblings. Some found this responsibility frustrating, such as a 62-year-old single man who retired in order to move to another state to care for his 90-year-old mother. He admits that "I feel a little *cheated*" as a consequence. And a 61-year-old unmarried woman says: "I had no intention of not continuing to work after retirement at 55 and the first two years I was solicited by friends for part-time jobs. After that, family commitments out of the city have prevented me from undertaking other responsibilities. I am not unhappy with my present lot, but think that if my 97-year-old mother died I might find more time on my hands, which I'd want to fill more productively than I have been doing."

A 66-year-old single woman writes at length about some of the burdens involved in caring for elderly relatives: "I anticipated a very rewarding retirement, having several hobbies, companionship, and a desire to travel and see old friends. Less than two days after I retired, my mother fell and has been an invalid ever since. My sister continued to work until last year, so that for three full years most of my time was taken up with caring for my mother. It now takes both my sister and myself to handle her and provide for her needs. I have little time for hobbies, have not had a vacation or even a weekend or overnight stay away from home in nearly four years. I have tried to get help through Medicaid and the local Nursing Association, but our combined incomes are over the limit for that type of assistance. On the other hand, if we hire someone to help, the cost would be prohibitive on our incomes. We feel that as long as we can care for her, we will not consider a nursing home."

Other retirees also describe their obligations. As a 70-year-old single woman puts it: "I am not free to travel or be away from home for very long. I have my 89-year-old mother to care for. I thank God every day that he gives me strength and patience to do this so that she won't have to go to a nursing home. I guess I would say I'm happy in my retirement." And a 68-year-old married man explains: "I am not free to take vacations and to travel with my wife because of an elderly, invalid mother. This is confining to both of us, and is an added strain on top of worry about a daughter who can't make a go of it completely on her own because of a physical handicap. These are not complaints. They are stated to show that retirement, even with adequate income, can be less than a time of complete happiness. I'm grateful that we can cope successfully with the problems that we did not expect to have to this degree." Some welcomed their obligation as an opportunity. "My retirement came at a very fortuitous time. I had an invalid sister and, shortly after, an invalid brother. It was a great relief to be able to devote time to both of them. I was very happy in my job at the university library and while I missed the associates and the work, I am sure I wouldn't have been able to cope successfully with both situations." A similar view comes from a 62-year-old man who welcomes the chance to "do work with others that need me. My mother, 82, and mother-in-law, 93, for example."

A 73-year-old widow offers this philosophical view: "Life is not, of course, perfect. What is living without some problems? I have a sister in a nursing home whom I visit weekly, a brother who has become an alcoholic, and a retarded nephew. But I also have 12 fine nephews and nieces as well as six living brothers and sisters."

Widows And Widowers

About 15% of our retirees had lost their spouses and, pre-dictably, the majority of the survivors were women. Of all the women in the survey, a quarter were widows; only 5% of the men in the survey were widowers. Although most widows and widowers rated themselves as "fairly" or "very" happy with life, those who chose to comment on their losses noted that they sorely missed their spouses. Indeed, many widows and widowers emphasize how utterly their lives in retirement had been trans-formed from what they expected.

A man age 86 says, "My wife died right after I retired so it changed my whole life pattern." Another man would otherwise have preferred to keep living near the college where he had worked, but "I knew my wife had only a short time to live, and I wanted her to have exactly what she wanted. My present environment is very pleasant but there are no people here with similar interests and background. They are pleasant, sterling characters— and rather dull. If only my wife had lived." According to a 71-year-old widow, "Life is never the same after you lose your mate and you never really get over it." An 83-year-old man writes, "Bring back my sweet 81-year-old wife I lost on May 5, 1982." And a 68-year-old man mourns, "We had a wonderful time together, and now I am alone."

A distraught 73-year-old bitterly dismisses previous retire-ment planning as futile: "We did plan, but my husband is gone, so what does it avail? Everything would be very very good if my husband were alive and well." And a 69-year-old widower says: "Had counted on my wife outliving me. I would not have put aside as much in retirement savings. The money would have done a lot more good if I spent it on my wife while she was alive." Several expressed the wish stated by this 69-year-old: "If I had known my husband was going to die, I would have retired several years sooner so that we could do some of the things we had wanted to do."

Retirement aggravated the loneliness created by being deprived of a spouse, especially when the two events occurred together. "Because my wife died shortly before I retired, I have had to adjust to living alone and retiring pretty much at the same time," says a 75-year-old. And some retirees vividly evoke the feeling of loneliness, such as this 85-year-old widower: "Current drawback has been loss of spouse as she was the spark plug of our social life. A big home and cooking is not meant for only one." Widows and widowers sometimes reproach themselves for not cultivating friends earlier to help compensate for the possible loss of a mate, such as this 72-year-old: "I would like to have developed more friends outside of the college, particularly since my husband died shortly after I retired. We had worked together in a sales business. I find it very hard to continue without his companionship." For the same reasons, some regret having forsaken the sociability of the workplace. Says a 68-year-old widow: "If I had realized how lonely it was going to be, I would have worked longer."

The widows and widowers write about how they have adjusted to the loss of a spouse. "My wife died the first year, when we were in the planning stage to take a trip, and so everything went under," says a 69-year-old man. "It took me a year and one half to get everything straightened out and it knocked the life out of one person." Yet, he vows, "I have now lived three years by myself and at times it is lonely, but I will keep on going as long as I last." Keeping active was popular advice. Counsels a 71-year-old whose husband died before retirement: "To keep very busy is the true answer to peace of mind, and at least limited happiness, in my situation. Just keep *busy* and be a part of the life around you!" Says another, "I do try to stay busy, keeping house and doing church work. I think everyone should take early retirement after years of work, and try to enjoy life at its fullest." Some, like the following 82-year-old, kept active by going back to a job. "I went to work to keep busy after losing my husband," she says.

Family relationships can also be an important way to cope with being thrust into the single life. A 77-year-old widower advises, "I recommend keeping up constant communication with your children, so that when you are old, or sick, or lose a life partner, you have children and grandchildren to share the sorrows of old age." To an 81-year-old: "Retirement was rewarding as my husband and myself worked most of our lives and we could visit our daughter, son-in-law, and six grandsons. Also we could go on trips and enjoy each other. When my husband had cancer and passed away it changed my life, but I still have lots of enjoyment from my family and now a great-granddaughter."

A few parlayed work and family together as a means of achieving the smoothest transition possible from a married to a single life, like this 79-year-old: "My life as a minister's wife was busy and enjoyable. When my husband died in 1961 after 35 years of marriage, there was an opening for a Latin teacher (my minor) and classes grew so that I had an assistant who taught three second-year (Caesar) classes. As my daughter was just entering high school I was very busy with keeping our home and teaching. As I have eight grandchildren and two great-grandchildren, I find family problems and responsibilities never end."

Yet another way for some retirees to come to grips with the loss of a spouse was to view this life-change in a larger perspective. Some draw sustenance for the present from the past, such as a 77-year-old man whose wife had died within the year and who writes: "It is hard to say that I am completely happy in my retirement, when I have to face up to living alone so unexpectedly. But I have absolutely no regrets and feel that I have been very lucky to have lived such a happy and productive life." A 69-year-old widow says, "Believing as I do that the acceptance of man's mortality and the understanding of the basic interrelatedness of all human experiences are fundamental to 'the good life,' I have been able to accept and enjoy the retirement experience," while a 73-year-old widow adds, "Life has a time for everything."

A 77-year-old man, whose wife had died within the year, comments that, "It is hard to say that I am completely happy in my retirement, when I have to face up to living alone so unexpectedly. But I have absolutely no regrets and feel that I have been very lucky to have lived such a happy and productive life." Says a woman: "Except for my husband being gone, I am a very happy 72." And according to a 77-year-old woman: "Our retirement is more rewarding due to the fact that my husband and I were together through nine of our retirement years. Who could ask for a greater reward than that?"

The Single Life

A third of the women retirees and a handful of the men had never married. Their comments reveal that some popular beliefs about singles may not be true. It is sometimes assumed, for example, that, compared to married people, lifelong singles would be more devoted to their jobs and the friendships those jobs created; it might therefore follow that singles would have a harder time getting used to retirement than marrieds. Actually, comments from never-married retirees indicate that most of them felt they made a smooth transition to retirement.

A woman aged 84 explains that in her working days: "I could mix community life with college life and with family life and build a very happy relationship with all three. When I retired I simply had more time for community and family. When someone remarked to me the September of my first retirement year, 'I guess you were fit to be tied when the school bells rang,' I replied, 'I didn't even know they had rung.' And as the weeks rolled on I wondered how I had ever found time to teach. In the 18 years of my retirement, I have continued to be interested and active and enjoy many of my former students as good friends, with whom I exchange many social courtesies." "When retirement comes," asserts a 79-year-old woman, "we find that we then have the time to find happiness if we just look for it among our friends and family."

It's also often assumed that single people might be particularly lonely, and some of our retirees clearly are, such as this 71-year-old woman. "There are certainly many compensations for being through with the working phases of my life. There are also many drawbacks, especially to one who is alone in retirement. Since I loved to work and got great satisfaction from my daily contact with young people and the constant challenge to my mind which comes from teaching, I miss my work terribly. I also miss the association with my college professor colleagues and the stimulation I received from the activities of a college community. Although I stay reasonably busy, for the first time in my life I am often overcome with loneliness. I wish I had become interested in something active like golf. Today, as I have for years, I get my exercise by a brisk two-mile walk every day, but this is a solitary activity. Although I do not care for bridge, I wish I had kept up with it enough to play now, primarily for the sociality of the game."

Nevertheless, only a handful specify loneliness as a complaint in their remarks on the drawbacks of retirement. Even fewer concede any regret over their single lives. There are exceptions, of course, such as a 79-year-old who says: "I would have accepted one of several proposals of marriage— companionship is important." But she tempers this confession with the observation that "there would be no guarantee of wedded bliss— and most of my friends are widows." She concludes, "I feel very fortunate in my retirement." According to the following retiree, "I would have married one of three women I loved, but they all had too many millions and I had seen other family men almost emasculated by it." Another man, age 61, alludes to a decision not to marry, but he does so with equanimity: "Possibly if I had married and had children decades before, retirement might be even more gratifying than it is now. But my working years could have been less satisfying if I'd had that dual life, and I might not yet be retired. However, it is hard for me, after only four years, to find anything that isn't rewarding in the retirement I have."

Despite generally lower incomes among singles than those who are married, single people did not express significantly more unhappiness over their economic well-being. But one exception directly blames the fact that she is single (and a woman) for her financial troubles. "Being an unmarried female," she writes, "you just have to take what an employer pays. On the whole, a female just does not get paid as much as a male. You do not have a spouse's insurance to count on. A single person gets caught in many ways. Some people are receiving Social Security who have never paid a dime into it. Such as: when husbands retire, their wives, who in most cases have never worked and paid into the plan, also receive a Social Security check. Women who have never married do not receive the same benefits. And my mother who lives with me and is 93 years old does not receive a Social Security check." A 72-year-old woman has another complaint: "In spite of a few loyal friends on whom I can count — unfortunately their number decreases every year through death — I often feel deprived of companionship, especially since practically everything here in the USA is geared to couples. If, for example, you have no choice but to travel alone you pay, at least in the Western Hemisphere, about a double amount. (Travel in Europe is somewhat better.) I believe a great deal could and ought to be done for widows and spinsters in this and other respects."

Probably because they lack the family bonds established by marriage, single retirees, particularly women, often maintain unusually strong attachments to their own kin, parents, and siblings. Friendships can be just as close as family ties. A 90-year-old woman congratulates herself on having "a house of my own choice, shared with a dear friend, and close to other friends and family." The financial as well as the social advantages of a similar arrangement appeal to another woman, age 87: "I found it very profitable to share with friends in buying a house before retirement and sharing equally in the expenses of home maintenance and living expenses."

Many of the never-married seem to exhibit a knack for making new friends, either to supplement or replace old ones. Perhaps the single life itself explains the apparent gift many of these people have for nurturing friendships; singles may simply have practiced more than married couples. A 69-year-old former math professor, for instance, who welcomed retirement notes the "opportunity to meet people and make new friends." A 69-year-old woman points out that "socializing with *non-academic* friends has been rewarding. The natural juices of academic people dry up. It is a pleasant change to meet and exchange ideas with people in other modes," while a 76-year-old woman who moved to be near her family observes that "it's very easy to become a part of the community." An 82-year-old woman says, "One important thing to remember is that we must be keenly aware of the value of new friends which we must be constantly making as our old friends begin leaving us." And a 79-year-old advises, "It is not a bad idea to shift to a somewhat different field of interest and thus become stimulated by new ideas and people," while a 77-year-old urges retirees to, "Do more entertaining. Lots of lonely and sad people in the world would appreciate a visit at your house."

Never-married retirees who enjoy rewarding friendships seem also to be more active in community service, which can provide the pleasures of socialization in addition to a sense of being useful. "I enjoy helping my older friends who need a car and occasional companionship. While I am able, I feel I owe a debt to my church, college, community, and family. So I serve where my abilities are needed," says a 69-year-old woman. Activities of all varieties, in fact, are emphasized by a great proportion of the single contingent, whether undertaken with others or alone. "There are so many things to do and always interesting persons to do them with," says one. Another, in contrast, explains, "Since I am inherently a home person, it's wonderful to have time to do all the things there was never enough time for — decorating, renovating, trying new recipes, entertaining. All the above is great because I'm not a social person. For one who is, the daily association with fellow employees and the bustle of the working world will probably be missed. I still keep in touch with the friends I made on the job, although mostly by telephone."

Single retirees stress self-reliance— of making do with one's inner resources— and self-assertiveness. Like a facility for making friends, this may be the product of a life without a marriage partner. A 66-year-old woman's remarks are typical: "I'm fortunate in that I do take the initiative. Sometimes it's not easy. There are letdowns and disappointments — but one must put forth some effort, explore, look for new horizons, etc. In the meantime, make the most of what is available."

Chapter 12—A MIX OF ATTRACTIONS AND DRAWBACKS

When our survey data — both the statistical portion and the volunteered comments that are the focus of this book — are examined as a whole, our retirees generally say they find retirement a satisfying experience. Nevertheless, there are aspects of retirement they are not all happy about. Previous chapters describe some of these troublesome things. The fact that retirement, as with life in general, is composed of both attractions and drawbacks comes through particularly clearly in those many cases where retirees gave us what amount to checklists of retirement's pros and cons.

Not everyone sees both sides, of course. Some retirees write about retirement solely in terms of attractions or drawbacks. Just a handful feel that retirement possesses no attractions at all, only drawbacks. An 82-year-old widower, for example, complains, "Until age 81, when serious illness emerged, leaving college employment did not bring 'retirement' in the ordinary sense. In the decade from age 70 to 80 I was fully employed in an executive capacity. Now, a host of difficulties have emerged and brought only the formality of emeritus status in employment, and a distressful and abrupt end to a way of life that had unfolded seamlessly up to this time." A larger number feel retirement has no drawbacks at all and write only about its attractions, such as the following 76-year-old man, who says: "Retirement has no drawbacks and I am enjoying it very much. This is attributable to the following factors: enough money, continuing professional interests, a miraculously happy second marriage, good health, living in an adult community with a complete program of activities available, a wonderful climate in Southern California."

Most of our retirees, however, write about both attractions

and drawbacks in retirement. To a certain extent, our retirees' comments were forced by the questions we asked. For example, perhaps some people do not feel strongly that retirement has drawbacks — but, because we specifically asked them to think in terms of attractions and drawbacks, they might have obliged by writing about *possible* drawbacks or about drawbacks that others might have experienced. The same applies, of course, to their comments about retirement's attractions.

Some retirees clearly couched their "drawbacks" in hypothetical terms, as applying more to others rather than themselves, such as this 74-year-old man:

"Drawbacks:

Some previously active persons cannot adjust to newfound leisure time.

More togetherness with spouse may create a problem.

Some previously successful, decision-making executive types find difficulty in adjusting to the 'leveling' process often experienced in retirement.

Attractions:

More leisure time to spend with spouse.

More opportunity to develop latent artistic and/or mechanical skills.

More opportunity to participate in public service activities with resultant feeling of usefulness to others.

More opportunities to travel.

More opportunities to participate in recreational activities, especially active sports."

For others, the "drawbacks" seem to cancel out their "attractions," like these listed by a man aged 63:

"Attractions	Drawbacks
(1) More time with family.	(1) Too much free time.
(2) Less tension personally.	(2) Frustration at being unemployed.
(3) Able to have more leisure time.	(3) Removal from a contributing position to one of inactivity."

A 74-year-old woman delights in feeling "free to speak more frankly to individuals" yet laments that "younger people think you are a 'has-been' and your advice or opinion doesn't amount to much." She also contrasts the fact that she has "more time for church and church work" with the complaint that "you are never selected for an important office in the church and other organizations." Often the aging process itself is enough to negate the attractions. "The main attraction turns out to be the main drawback," says a 74-year-old widower, who continues, "Unfortunately, retirement and getting older come together and for many the latter means aches and pains which seriously interfere with the enjoyment of most retirement opportunities. If I'd been in good health I'd have had a ball."

For the most part, our retirees tended to view retirement's "pros" and "cons" as complementary, as good and bad aspects of a single situation. One man, for example, counterbalances "diminished social or professional contacts with colleagues whose friendship I value" with "freedom from contact with uncongenial colleagues." Here is a longer sample from a widow aged 66:

"Attractions	Drawbacks
(1) No job pressure.	(1) Miss daily contact with people.
(2) More time to take care of business and errands at convenient times.	(2) Miss challenge of work and money.
(3) More rest and time for recreation and hobbies.	(3) Lonely at times.
(4) More time to spend with family — some for giving assistance, some just for fun.	(4) Not as much contact.
(5) Can travel and go places during the week instead of on weekends when everyone else is rushing around and places are crowded.	(5) Easy to sit around too much unless you get into an exercise program."

She sums up some of the major contrasts we already examined: the release from the more unpleasant demands of work versus the absence of its rewards; the chance to spend more time with family at the price of a loss of contacts with colleagues and the young; the new freedom of choice together with its enticements to laziness. Another retiree recognizes this pattern in his own reactions when, regretting the "loss of many real pleasures in teaching and studying," he realizes that this loss "is, clearly, the mirror image of the 'attractions.' One can't have it both ways."

In opposing "attractions" to "drawbacks," our retirees very often cited the "newness" of the opportunities provided by retirement as examples of both. For instance, one woman reports that she likes being able to "make new friends and associates in areas and fields new to you." At the same time she also warns that it is "more difficult to make new friends as one grows older" — a difficulty compounded in her case by a move to a new locality, which she now sees as a mistake. A man aged 69 compares his freedom "to develop new activities" with his "need to develop new contacts and acquaintances in other fields of interest" as the means toward this end.

Retirement provides time for all sorts of new pastimes, but capitalizing on this time takes work, observes a 75-year-old woman. She writes:

"Attractions

(1) Opportunity to broaden types of people-contacts. Previously strictly limited to academic types, I began to know farm people, business people, etc.

(2) Opportunity and time to explore unknown fields. One can either take courses in totally unexplored field or do volunteer work in a strange field, etc.

Drawbacks

(1) One tends to lose people-contacts and become isolated over the years. People-contacts are something that one can not expect to be spontaneous but have to *work* at.

(2) It takes constant effort to maintain intellectual level. One's field changes and does *not* stay as one knew it."

Similarly, the chance to do "community service" is commonly mentioned as one of the pleasures of retirement. But this new opportunity may also have a nuisance side to it. Says an 80-year-old man: "I'm being constantly bombarded with requests to be on this or that committee, or to do this or that volunteer work beyond that which others will do, or because they won't do it, without regard to my wishes. People do not respect my freedom, my time, or my state of mind. Their justification for their action is 'you have so much time now you can begin being a citizen of this city' (as if I had not been one while I was working)."

A 67-year-old man has this view: "It is generally recognized that a working person's time is committed to his job and his 'free' time is pretty well confined to home and family. On the other hand, a retiree is generally regarded as having no demands upon his time and so is subject to call to do this, that, and the other thing. This leads at first, to over-involvement in a variety of causes and organizations. A person has to learn to get out of this 'rat race,' which in some respects is more vicious than the one of working years. This is the negative side. The positive is that a person has an opportunity to keep busy and to shop for what is most important to him and end up with a pace and degree of involvement that suits him."

Indeed, the fact that retirement life is an amalgam of things was emphasized by a 73-year-old woman who chose to answer our question with the simple statement: "I find it impossible to list the drawbacks of retirement— because aren't they identical with the rewards?"

Chapter 13: A SUMMING UP

Retirement, for most of us, is inevitable. Yet many working people are not sure what lies ahead for them in this next phase of their lives and there is probably a tendency to think about retirement in terms of stereotypes. At one extreme is the "golden years" vision — a time of harvesting the fruits of a working career and, free from bosses, commuting, and timeclocks, of romping with the grandchildren when one isn't traveling or engaged in stimulating, long-postponed activities. The opposite stereotype is dominated by images of wrinkles, canes, wheelchairs, paltry incomes, and eroding intellects. The whole business is more complicated than that, as probably most people suspect without being quite sure how.

We hope this book helps replace the stereotypes with the vivid experiences of real people, particularly in regard to not-so-obvious aspects of retirement. We have tried to do this by letting our retirees describe in their own words retirement's many dimensions, as they have experienced them. As such, this has been a book about individuals and that means that not all of our retirees' comments, feelings, and suggestions are applicable to every reader of this book. But much of what's here undoubtedly will be helpful, and at the very least these experiences should serve as guideposts as the reader forms his or her own expectations about retirement.

Our retirees tell us that like full-time work and probably any other aspect of our lives, the retirement experience can be a blend of both the pleasant and unpleasant— opportunity and pitfall, joy and tedium, challenge and drudgery, rewarding social experiences and those decidedly otherwise. There is another message that permeates these comments: while there are things most of us cannot control, the precise balance of these and other factors depends in good part on how (and how much) we prepare for this new lifestyle.

The need for preparation is so important because, as our retirees so vividly describe, retirement can be a drastic life-change. What's more, for most of us retirement coincides with another drastic life-change: older age. These are years that represent a new and quite different phase of our lives and one that, given the trend toward earlier retirements and longer lifespans, can easily last 20 or more years— a quarter or more of a lifetime.

Based on our retirees' comments, preparation for retirement, at its roots, actually involves some rather simple notions:

Build up retirement savings. Income from Social Security and employer pensions may be quite adequate, but the greater the financial resources you can draw on the greater your ability to react to the unexpected or simply to shape retirement the way you want to. One way to build up retirement funds is to save regularly. Furthermore, extra savings are possible by taking advantage of tax-deferral opportunities, such as those provided by Individual Retirement Accounts (IRAs) and tax-deferred annuities for employes of nonprofit institutions.

Get first-hand knowledge of people and places. Perhaps the best knowledge comes from people who have been there already. In recounting the experiences of retired people, this book can be a starting point for developing the questions to pose to other retired colleagues about what you are likely to encounter in both the transition to retirement and retirement itself. First-hand knowledge is particularly helpful if you are thinking of relocating. Our retirees suggest sampling an area in advance, possibly by spending vacations there or even renting before buying a home. They suggest as well talking to people who live (or lived) there about their reactions to moving away from friends and relatives, what your potentially new neighbors may be like, the adequacy of social, library, cultural, medical, and even supermarket facilities, and so on.

Tap the specialists. Take advantage of retirement counseling opportunities— formal planning may help organize your thoughts and you can hear what your colleagues are thinking about.

Retirement specialists can bolster your knowledge in areas you are weak in and pass along tips and the experiences of others. Read about retirement and old age (although the quality of available materials varies).

Ask questions of yourself. How will you compensate for the changes in a lifestyle that most of us have been used to for almost 50 years? Retirement provides relief from the unwelcome aspects of work, of course, but at the same time a large part of our life-structure is tailored by our jobs — daily routines, the network of friends and professional colleagues, access to professional resources and facilities, the prestige and community status derived from your institutional role and related sense of self-worth, a sense of mission and working with others toward a common goal. To smooth the process, some retirees suggest exploring the possibility of going from full-time work to full-time retirement in stages.

Involve your spouse. If you are married, retirement inevitably involves both you and your spouse. Where a wife is younger than her husband, for example, she may want to continue her career and not retire when her husband does, possibly disappointing some of his retirement plans. Whether one or both are retired, spouses may have to develop new daily routines — a process that may be initially irksome. Spouses may also need to develop realistic expectations of what to expect from each other as the ties with former colleagues, and the related social and intellectual stimulation, weaken. Such potential tensions can best be defused ahead of time by cooperatively thinking through retirement's possibilities.

Take action far ahead of actual retirement. In the case of personal savings, a long time frame allows you to take advantage of the regular accumulation of savings and compounding of earnings; regular saving, no matter how small, can yield impressive results over long periods of time. In the nonfinancial area, time enables you to gather and absorb as much information as possible — and increases the chances of uncovering key nuggets of information.

View retirement in perspective. Some people perceive retirement in a negative way because of coincidental age-related factors, such as aging itself and declining energy levels. Obviously, age-related changes will occur whether you retire or not.

Retirement, in short, has the potential to be a substantial, uplifting part of one's life and deserves to be eagerly anticipated. As a 61-year-old widow puts it: "Retirement is a very valuable time of life. There is time to know and grow in a different way."

Chapter 14: THE QUESTIONNAIRE

Teachers
Insurance and
Annuity
Association

College
Retirement
Equities
Fund

730 Third Avenue
New York
NY 10017
(212) 490-9000

ANNUITANT
SURVEY

1982 Survey of TIAA-CREF Annuitants

SPECIAL INSTRUCTIONS:

1. Please do not sign your name to the questionnaire. To assure that all information will remain confidential, we want respondents to be anonymous.

2. Please complete and return the questionnaire only if you are now retired or, if now employed, previously had retired from your main occupation.

3. If you have never retired, please do not fill out the questionnaire, but check this box instead ☐ and then return the questionnaire so that we can count the people in your category.

4. Most questions can be answered simply by checking the box alongside the statement that best fits your situation or your opinion. Only a few questions require filling in numbers or writing a brief response.

Ten years ago we conducted a comprehensive study of retired TIAA-CREF annuitants to obtain first-hand reports of their retirement situations. The cooperation of the people surveyed was extraordinary, and the study provided a considerable amount of useful information. Among other things, we have used this information in the development of retirement planning seminars that we now conduct throughout the country for participants and their spouses who are nearing retirement age.

Not much is constant in this rapidly changing world, including the experiences of people in retirement. So we are surveying today's retired TIAA-CREF annuitants to learn how they are faring. You are one of a group selected at random to represent all TIAA-CREF annuitants. By completing and returning this questionnaire you will be giving us current information that we can use to assess

our services, our retirement planning seminars, and our communications with participants retired and not yet retired.

We will be most grateful to you for taking the time to fill out and return the questionnaire. Please try to answer all the questions and then return the completed form in the postage-paid envelope we have provided. We hope your effort will be rewarded by the knowledge that you are participating in a study to benefit present and future generations of retirees.

James Mulanaphy

James Mulanaphy
Study Director

P.S. If you want additional information about the study, please call me (collect, if long distance) at (212) 490-9000, extension 2291.

PART I: Retirement Plans and Preparation
Note: All percentages are on a base of 1,794 unless otherwise indicated.

---

1. At what age did you retire (first retirement if more than one)?

8%	Under 60	33%	65
20	60-62	20	66-69
11	63-64	8	70 and older

---

2. Did you retire by choice or were there factors beyond your control that forced you to retire?

67% Retired by choice (ANSWER Q2a-b)

33   Did not retire by choice (GO TO Q2c)

—   Other (Please specify):

If you did retire by choice, please answer 2a-b below.

2a. What was the main reason you retired when you did? (Please check all that apply)

(n = 1,208)
46% Had planned to retire at that age

13   Unhappy with work situation

3   Not performing the job up to my expectations

29   Retirement income was sufficient to do so

34   Felt it was time to retire

10   Spouse retired then

23   Wanted more time for self and/or family

33   Wanted to do other things besides work

5   Health

3   Family responsibility

3   Took a different job

2b) If you could do it over, would you still retire at the same age, retire at a younger age, or retire at an older age?

(n = 1,208)
67% Retire at same age

11   Retire at younger age

12   Retire at older age

8   Not certain

2   No response

If you did Not retire by choice, please answer 2c below.

2c) Why did you retire when you did?

(n = 581)
63% Reached employer's mandatory retirement age

15   Was forced by administration

9   Was disabled

8   Poor health

Other (Please specify):

5   Budget cutbacks/position eliminated

3. As best as you can recall, how did you feel about the prospect of your retiring just before you actually did retire?

- 58% Was looking forward to retiring
- 16 Was neutral about retiring
- 18 Disliked the idea of retiring
- 6 Not certain
- 2 No response

4. Did your last employer offer employees counseling or other assistance in personal planning for retirement (other than providing a pension plan)?

- 21% Yes
- 74 No
- 4 Not certain
- 1 No response

If you answered Yes to this question, please answer 4a below.

(n = 374)

4a) Did you receive pre-retirement planning assistance from your employer?

- 74% Yes (Please describe the help you received)
  (n = 278)
  - 42% seminar   25% other
  - 21 One-to-one counseling   7 No response
  - 5 Printed material
- 5 Assistance not offered to you
- 18 Declined assistance
- 3 No response

5. Looking back at your own planning for retirement, how thorough a job of preparing for retirement would you say you did?

- 35% Very thorough
- 48 Some, but not thorough
- 12 Did not plan at all for retirement
- 3 Not certain
- 2 No response

6. Is there any area of retirement planning that you now wish you had given more attention?

- 29% Yes (Please indicate what area this is)
  (n = 521)
  - 31% Finances/income   8% Hobbies
  - 17 Investments   8 Housing
  - 13 TIAA-CREF pension   7 Working after retiring
- 54 No
- 12 Not certain
- 5 No response

7. In general, how satisfied are you now with the preparations you made for retirement?

- 36% Very satisfied
- 51 Reasonably satisfied
- 8 Not satisfied
- 3 Not certain
- 2 No response

8. In your opinion, do you feel participation in a formal retirement preparation program before retiring would be useful to most workers?

71% Yes

5   No

22 Not certain

2   No response

9. In general, how satisfied are you with your retirement?

51% Very satisfied

41 Reasonably satisfied

5   Not satisfied

1   Not certain

2   No response

PART II: Retirement Activities

10. Before retiring, did you expect to work for salary or other compensation after you retired?

28% Yes
63 No
9   Not certain

11. Since retiring, have you ever worked for salary or other compensation?

45% Yes (ANSWER 11a-e)
55 No (GO TO 11f)

If you answered Yes to question 11, please answer 11a-e below.

11a) Are you presently working for salary or other compensation?

21% Yes
79 No

(n = 801)

11b) Is (was) your work after retirement part-time or full-time?

80% Part-time
16 Full-time
3   Other (Please specify):
1   No response

(n = 801)

11c) What kind of work do (did) you do? (Please describe briefly)

25% Teaching   25% Other profes-
                           sional work
17 Consulting   12 Office work/retail
                           sales
6   Writing   7   Manual work

(n = 801)

11d) Was your main reason for working after you retired mostly non-financial or financial?

52% Combination of non-financial and financial
34 Non-financial only, e.g., enjoying working, wanted to do something
12 Financial only, e.g., wanted extra money
—   Other (Please specify):
2   No response

(n = 801)

11e) Did you have much difficulty finding suitable work after you retired?

9% Yes (Please indicate what the difficulty was)
(n = 74)
32% No jobs   10% Other
28 Age   26 No response
4   Skills

88% No
3   No response

If you answered No to question 11, please answer 11f below.

(n = 988)

11f) Have you looked for paid work since retiring?

5% Yes
92 No
3   No response

12. Since retiring, have you been involved with any unpaid voluntary or charitable activity?

50% Yes (ANSWER 12a-c)

50   No (GO TO 12d)

If you answered Yes to question 12, please answer 12a-c below.

12a) Are you presently doing unpaid voluntary or charitable activity?

(n = 891)
76% Yes

22   No

2   No response

12b) How many hours a week do (did) you normally devote to such activity?

(n = 891)
41% 5 or less
25   6-10
17   More than 10
17   No response

12c) What kind of voluntary or charitable activity do (did) you do? (Please describe briefly)

(n = 891)
28% Community/civic

27   Educational/cultural

26   Church related

15% Hospital/health service

13   Helping the elderly

11   Non-specific

If you answered No to question 12, please answer 12d below.

12d) Have you looked into doing unpaid voluntary or charitable activity since retiring?

(n = 893)
8% Yes

86   No

6   No response

---

13. Listed below and on the next page are a number of activities. Which do you presently pursue? For each activity, please check the YES box if you are involved with it or the NO box if you are not.

ACTIVITIES	PRESENTLY YES	PURSUE NO	NO RESPONSE
1. Gardening and/or home improvement work	71%	28	1
2. Hobbies and/or crafts	61%	38	1
3. Attending a formal or informal educational program	28%	71	1

ACTIVITIES	PRESENTLY YES	PURSUE NO	No Response
4. Participating in sports or a physical fitness program	33%	66	1
5. Recreational travel	66%	33	1
6. Community service and/or political activity	35%	64	1
7. Participation in a professional association or other occupational-related organization	32%	67	1
8. Participation in a civic, fraternal or other formal group	31%	68	1
9. Participation in a retirees' club or organization	23%	76	1
10. Socializing with friends on a regular basis	75%	24	1
11. Religious or church activity (other than attendance and services)	37%	62	1
12. Writing, painting, or other creative pursuit	43%	56	1
13. Reading	92%	7	1

14. **Is there one of these activities (or more) that your especially enjoy doing?**

83% Yes (Please specify the activity(ies))
(n = 1,481)

38%	Reading	22%	Creative pursuits
27	Hobbies/crafts	20	Gardening/home improvements
26	Recreational travel	15	Sports/physical fitness
		15	Socializing with friends

11 No

6 No response

PART III: Housing and Location

15. Do you own or rent your home?

72% Own house (ANSWER 15a)

6   Own condominium or cooperative unit (ANSWER 15a)

15   Rent apartment

3   Rent house

4   Other (Please specify):

If you own your home, please answer 15a below.

15a) Do you make mortgage payments on it?

(n = 1,397)

23% Yes (Please indicate how many more years you are scheduled to make payments)

(n = 318)

25% 5 or less   33% 11-20

25   6-10   17   More than 20

72   No

5   No response

16. All things considered, would you prefer to continue living in your present home or would you prefer to move somewhere else?

83% Prefer to stay in present home

10   Prefer to move (Please indicate why)

(n = 188)

21% More suitable home   10% Be nearer family

19   Better climate   7   Reduce maintenance

16   Safer area

5   Not certain

2   No response

17. Do you share your home with anyone or live alone?

57% Live with spouse only

8   Live with spouse and another (others)

24   Live alone

10   Live with another (others); no spouse

1   No response

18. How many years have you lived in your present home?

27% 5 or less

16   6-10

24   11-20

32   More than 20

1   No response

19. Is your present home the one you lived in before you retired?

57% Yes

43   No (ANSWER 19a-c)

If you answered No to question 19, please answer 19a-c below.

19a) Did you move at or about the time you retired or did you move later?

(n = 770)

59% Moved at or about retirement

39   Moved later

2   No response

19b) Do you now live in the same area as you did before retiring?

(n = 770)

22% Yes

73   No

5   No response

19c) What was the main reason you moved?

(n = 770)

29% A better climate

17   To live in a nicer area

30   To be nearer family or friends

16   To get a home of more appropriate size

9   Health

17   Reduce home maintenance responsibilities

15   Reduce cost of maintaining home

12   Reduce property tax

Other (Please specify)

4   Took a new job

3   Moved to a retirement community

2   Already owned home

2   No response

PART IV: Financial Aspects of Retirement

20. Listed below are various sources of retirement income. Please indicate by checking the appropriate box in Column 1 the sources from which you do or do not currently receive income. In addition, please give your best estimate of the percentage of total retirement income coming from each source by entering the percent figures in Column 2. (These figures should total to 100%). If married, include any income your spouse receives.

RETIREMENT INCOME SOURCES	**1** Receive Income From Source			**2** Percentage of Total Income From Source		
	Yes	No	No Response			
1. TIAA and/or CREF annuities	98%	0	2	(n = 1,428)	26% 21 26 27	1%-5% 6%-10% 11%-20% More than 20%
2. Social Security	94%	4	2	(n = 1,356)	25% 28 26 21	1%-20% 21%-33% 34%-50% More than 50%
3. Other pension (e.g., state retirement system)	48%	50	2	(n = 751)	26% 29 23 22	1%-10% 11%-25% 26%-40% More than 40%
4. Individual Retirement Account (IRA), personal Tax-Deferred Annuity (TDA or SRA) or Keogh plan	7%	91	2	(n = 107)	25% 24 27 24	1%-2% 3%-5% 6%-10% More than 10%
5. Current employment, including consulting or professional practice	22%	76	2	(n = 338)	25% 28 25 22	1%-5% 6%-15% 16%-33% More than 33%
6. Interest or dividends on savings, stocks, etc.	82%	16	2	(n = 1,234)	28% 27 22 23	1%-10% 11%-25% 26%-40% More than 40%
7. Drawing down savings, other annuities, life insurance, or other assets.	15%	83	2	(n = 217)	25% 22 23 30	1%-2% 3%-5% 6%-10% More than 10%
8. Other (e.g., royalties, rental income)	20%	78	2	(n = 308)	16% 24 37 23	1%-2% 3%-5% 6%-20% More than 20%

21. Is any other person besides yourself (and spouse, if married) mainly supported by your household income?

8% Yes

85　No

7　No response

22. Considering all sources, please check the income category indicating the total annual income of your household for 1981 (before taxes and other deductions). If married, include any income your spouse receives.

2%	Less than $ 5,000	12%	$20,001-$25,000
3	$ 5,000-$ 7,500	10	$25,001-$30,000
5	$ 7,501-$10,000	8	$30,001-$35,000
8	$10,001-$12,500	6	$35,001-$40,000
8	$12,501-$15,000	10	$40,001-$50,000
12	$15,001-$20,000	10	More than $50,000
		6	No response

23. Considering both income and expenses, how well would you say you are living?

27% Very well
37 Well
31 Adequately
3 Not too well
2 No response

24. Compared to when you retired, how do you feel your overall financial situation in general is now—better, worse, or about the same?

28% Better now
17 Worse now
50 About the same
3 Not certain
2 No response

25. Giving your best estimate, how does your current total income compare to your total income before you retired?

Compared to preretirement income, current income is:
26% More
25 About the same
9 Over three-quarters
10 About three-quarters
7 About two-thirds
7 Between half and two-thirds
7 About half
2 Between one-third and half
2 One-third or less
5 No response

26. Since you retired, have you regularly taken money from your savings or sold securities or other property to meet current expenses (but not to purchase something special)?

12% Yes
84 No
2 No savings or investments
2 No response

27. Since you retired, have you had to make any adjustments in your life style because of increases in the cost of living?

29% Yes (Please specify the adjustment(s))
(n = 527)

33%	Less travel	16%	Buying less clothes
23	Less dining out	15	Not buying as much
20	Cutting back extras	15	Cutting back basics
		12	No response

68 No
3 No response

PART V: TIAA-CREF Participation

The questions in this section cover aspects of your participation in the TIAA-CREF system both before you retired and after you started to receive annuity income.

28. Giving your best estimate, in what year did you first enter the TIAA-CREF retirement system?

6% Before 1940
13 1940's
23 1950's
35 1960's
13 1970's
10 No reponse

29. For how many years since then until you retired did your employer(s) make contributions to your TIAA-CREF annuity?

13% 1-5
23 6-10
18 11-15
11 16-20
8 21-25
11 More than 25
16 No response

30. What year did you begin to receive your TIAA-CREF annuity income?

3% Before 1965
9 1965-1969
21 1970-1974
35% 1975-1979
27 1980-1982
5 No response

31. When arranging to begin your TIAA-CREF annuity income, were you satisfied with the service provided by TIAA-CREF at that time?

75% Very satisfied
15 Somewhat satisfied
5 Not satisfied (Please indicate why)
2 Not certain
3 No response

32. When the actual amount of monthly income you would first receive from your TIAA-CREF annuity was determined, was it about what you expected it would be?

45% Yes
26 No, somewhat less
6 No, somewhat more
13 Had not thought about it beforehand
8 Not certain
2 No response

PART VI: General Information

The questions in this section request information that will enable us to learn how groups of respondents with similar characteristics differ or are the same in the ways they have experienced and reacted to retirement.

---

33. Please indicate:

a) Your present age

11%	60-64	18%	75-79
33	65-69	7	80-84
29	70-74	2	85 and older

b) Your sex

60% Male

40　Female

c) Your present marital status

65% Married

14　Widowed

16　Never married

5　Separated or divorced

d) How many living children you have

30% None

14　One

25　Two

16　Three

11　Four or more

4　No response

If you are presently married, please answer questions 34-36 (n = 1,169)

34. What is your spouse's age?

8%	Under 60	14%	75-79
18	60-64	4	80-84
32	65-69	1	85 and older
23	70-74		

---

35. What is your spouse's present employment status?

64% Fully retired

8　Partially retired, employed part-time

7　Employed full-time

17　Never employed

3　Other (Please specify)

1　No response

---

36. Is your spouse receiving or expecting to receive a pension or annuity (other than Social Security) based on his or her own employment?

40% Yes

58　No

1　Not certain

1　No response

37. In general, how would you describe your health (and that of your spouse, if you are married) in relation to others your age?

YOURSELF		SPOUSE (n = 1,169)	
22%	Excellent	18%	Excellent
29	Very good	29	Very good
37	Good	33	Good
9	Poor	11	Poor
2	Very poor	2	Very poor
1	No response	7	No response

38. How is your health now compared to your health in recent years?

64%	About the same
8	Better now
23	Not as good now
4	Much worse now
1	No response

39. Are you in the Medicare program of Social Security?

18%	Yes, Part A only (hospital insurance)
70	Yes, Part A and Part B (supplementary medical insurance)
11	No
—	Not certain
1	No response

40. Do you have any other health insurance coverage, either group or individual, besides Medicare?

28%	Yes, under individual policy purchased by self
51	Yes, under group plan of former employer (yours or spouse's) or other organization
11	Yes, under both own policy and group plan
9	No
—	Not certain
1	No response

41. How would you describe your overall health insurance coverage?

26%	Very good
57	Adequate
10	Less than adequate
2	Poor
4	Not certain
1	No response

42. **What kind of work did you do during your working career (main occupation if more than one)?**

38% College-level teaching

6 Elementary or secondary school teaching

12 College-level management or administration

2 Elementary or secondary school management or administration

22 Other professional or technical work, (e.g., accountant, engineer, librarian, physician)

20 Support specialist (e.g., craftsman, payroll assistant, secretary)

— Other (Please specify)

43. **What type of organization did you work for at the time of your retirement?**

70% College or university

9 Primary, intermediate, or secondary school

5 Educational service organization other than a teaching institution

6 Research organization

3 Hospital

6 Non-educational organization (e.g., bank, industrial firm, government agency, law firm)

1 Other (Please specify)

44. **Taking all things together, would you say you are now generally very happy with life, fairly happy or not too happy?**

55% Very happy

38 Fairly happy

4 Not too happy

3 No response

Thank you for your help. Please return the completed questionnaire in the enclosed postage-paid envelope.